Beetlemania

Beetlemania

The Story of the Car that Captured the Hearts of Millions

Kate McLeod

SMITHMARK

Dedicated to Volkswagen, for building the New Beetle and putting the smiles back into driving; to J. Mays, Freeman Thomas, and the design team who brilliantly reinvented this icon; and to Jerry Flint, whose wisdom, knowledge, and love has made me a better person and a better writer.

This edition published in 1999 by SMITHMARK Publishers, a division of U.S. Media Holdings, Inc., 115 West 18th Street, New York, NY 10011.

SMITHMARK books are available for bulk purchase for sales promotion and premium use. For details, write or call the manager of special sales, SMITHMARK Publishers, 115 West 18th Street, New York, NY 10011; 212-519-1300.

Designed by Galen Smith

Edited by Marisa Bulzone

Editorial Director: Elizabeth Sullivan

ISBN: 0-7651-1018-0

10 9 8 7 6 5 4 3 2 1

Library of Congress Cataloging-in-Publication Data
McLeod, Kate, 1944–
    Beetlemania : the story of the car that captured
    the hearts of millions / Kate McLeod.
        p.   cm.
    ISBN 0–7651–1018–0
    1. Volkswagen Beetle automobile--History.   I. Title.
    TL215.V6M39   1999
    629.222'2--dc21   98–49790
                                                                           CIP

Printed in Hong Kong

Acknowledgments

I would like to thank the following people for their encouragement, for opening up their libraries, their files, their memories, and their memento drawers. Steve Keyes, Director of Corporate Communication, and Tony Fouladpour, Public Relations Manager at Volkswagen of America, and all the other people at Volkswagen who plowed through the files looking for old photos; Tom McDonald, Vice President, Public Affairs, at The Budd Company, a former Volkswagen public relations man who entrusted me with important documents from his Volkswagen collection and sent me several books that were very helpful; Baron Bates, also formerly of Volkswagen public relations, who gave me leads, anecdotes, and lent me materials; Ken Zino at Ford Motor Company; Greg Merksamer; all of the auto journalists who chatted with me about the project and wished me well; Art Railton, former head of public relations at Volkswagen, who shared his wonderful memories with me; and Walter Henry Nelson, author of *Small Wonder*, the lovingly created, detailed history of the Beetle that was an inspiration to me all through this project. I also thank Doyle Dane Bernbach, creators of the original Volkswagen advertising, and The Arnold Agency, creators of the current New Beetle campaign, for their help in securing prints of the ads. Finally, thanks to Marisa Bulzone, my editor, for entrusting me with this project, and to Galen Smith, my designer, for taking such good care of my first book.

Contents

Introduction

The Beetle was reborn on January 5, 1998, at the North American Auto Show in Detroit.

People jammed the display, their necks craning to get that first glimpse. The automotive press, nor-

mally a crusty bunch, wrote articles dripping with praise. They cooed about the styling, driveability, and

pricing. When the New Beetle went on sale two months later, it took America by storm. Consumers lined up,

and once again, they bought it in droves. ✳ Reincarnation means you come back, but not in the same form as

before. The New Beetle is truly a Beetle, but it's different in almost every way than it was before. It is heavier and longer than

the old Beetle; its four-cylinder or Turbo Direct Injection diesel engine is located in the front of the car—not at the rear; and the engine is water-cooled,

not air-cooled. Not only does the New Beetle have a heater and air-conditioner that work, but also a six-speaker stereo with a CD-player, cup holders, halo-

gen headlights, and four-wheel disc brakes. It even holds the road when the wind blows or a Semi passes. ✳ Its designers swear it isn't retro, that it's based

instead on the shape considered to be the most perfect—the circle. Is it the purity of the circle that makes our hearts leap when we see this car—or is it the

memories? Retro or no, this new car takes its emotional cues from the heart of the old Beetle. ✳ Owners of the New Beetle had to be startled by public

reaction "Complete strangers stick   their heads in the car to look," says

one New Yorker who   handed her yellow 1974

1968 Volkswagen Sedan

Beetle, nicknamed Chitty, over to a

friend and bought a New Beetle in silver. "Before you know it, they're sitting

right beside you in the passenger seat. It's an interesting way to meet people." ✳ "The best

thing about the New Beetle is that women tell you what they did in the old one," says Ken Gross, Director of

the Petersen Automotive Museum in Los Angeles. ✳ Anecdotes are as much a part of the character of the Beetle as

its size, shape, and pugnacious personality. On an early New Beetle test drive from New York to Washington, my husband and

I experienced life as royalty. We waved, smiled, and held our thumbs up for four solid hours. Someone driving a Ryder rental truck

on the New Jersey Turnpike took our picture as he held the steering wheel with one hand and swerved along the highway. Another fel-

low traveler raced his BMW into a parking space next to ours at the Turnpike rest area, leapt out of his car, composed himself, and said in a

controlled voice, "How do you like it?" ✳ Volkswagen means "people's car" in German and the car lives up to its name in the truest sense. It's completely

approachable, like an old friend. People lose their inhibitions around it: We found a family of Italian tourists posed around the car taking snap-

shots in a New York parking lot. The parking atten-

dant was elated that the car was

1970 Volkswagen Sedan

1969 Volkwagen Sedan

attracting so much attention—cars were pulling in just to see the

New Beetle. ✳ Given its lovable nature, it is hard to imagine a stranger or darker

beginning. Born in facism, the Beetle became a symbol and a facilitator of freedom, particularly in

America. (It was in the U.S. that it got the names Bug and Beetle; the Germans called it the Type 1.) An

uncommon alliance between Europe's greatest automobile designer and history's most evil dictator gave the

car its start. Yet, no company has so consistently had the right people at the helm at the right time—all of them

brilliant. Volkswagen was lucky that way. Each of the men who contributed to the success of the old Beetle were very dif-

ferent in style and substance, but they made the Beetle what it is—a car that's hugged around the world. ✳ The history of the Beetle is the most

fascinating of any car ever built. It is the most famous, the most recognized car in the world—and emotion has played a large part in the creation of the

legend. Call it love—the custom paint jobs, the modifications, the races, the contests, the flotillas. The Beetle even had its own film career, and you can

be sure that Volkswagen never paid a fee to have its product placed in a movie. ✳ Thanks to this New Beetle, there's a New Beetle era and people are

smiling on the highways again. Bankers are making headlines stuffing themselves into a New Beetle trying to break a 1969 record. Bankers, not college

students. This is not your father's Oldsmobile—or his Volkswagen. It's already begun to create its own legends. ✳ Old or new, there's one

thing for sure about the Beetle: It's more than a cult; it is a culture.

THE BIRTH OF
THE BEETLE

In February 1933, the Berlin Auto Show served as the first public forum for Adolph Hitler, the new Chancellor of Germany. Hitler, a car buff who never learned to drive, promised the audience he would build a great network of highways in Germany; it was to be called the autobahn. He vowed to reduce the automobile taxes, ease the traffic laws, and make it easier to obtain drivers' licenses.

Hitler had been imprisoned in the Landsberg Fortress in 1923. He spent his time writing *Mein Kampf* and reading a biography of Henry Ford. Inspired by Ford and the burgeoning American auto industry, Hitler envisioned a Germany where everyone could own a car. German auto makers, who had little interest in building a small, unprofitable car, took his promises to be a campaign maneuver. They were wrong.

The idea for such a car had been in the air for many years. Auto designer Ferdinand Porsche had developed several Beetle-like test cars for different German manufacturers—constantly testing, retesting, and reworking his ideas. By the time he met the person who would help him realize his dream, Porsche was fifty-three years old.

Hitler had seen Porsche's document calling for the construction of the *Kleinauto* (little car). They met at the Kaiserhof Hotel in Berlin, supposedly for only fifteen minutes. Porsche sketched his

Alternately called Project 12, Volksauto, and Kleinauto, this precursor to the Beetle was designed by Porsche in 1932 and built for Zundapp Motorcycle Works by The Porsche Bureau, Porsche's independent consulting firm. *Inset:* The last prototype built before the KdF car was the Type 60W30. Thirty were built. Each vehicle was driven 80,000 test miles.

ideas for a small car and listened as Hitler added his thoughts. Porsche could meet the Fuhrer's requirements for design and performance and the Fuhrer could singlehandedly realize Porsche's vision of producing a small, cheap car.

Production was to be funded by the German Auto Dealers' Association (RDA), not the Third Reich. Although German auto makers were not enthusiastic, they had little choice. Reluctantly, they drew up a contract for Porsche.

The cost of the Volkswagen's testing and development was far beyond what any private company could have afforded. The first three cars tested were hand-tooled by Porsche

and his devoted staff, working out of Porsche's garage at his Stuttgart design studio. He received little or no help from German auto makers beyond financing. At the Auto Show in January 1935, Hitler announced that the German people would see the first cars tested by the middle of the year. But Porsche, who was always late and over budget, did not meet the terms of his contract—no cars were tested in 1935. When Hitler spoke at the Auto Show in 1936, his speech was broadcast to every motor-vehicle and auto-accessories plant in Germany. He said the day was close at hand when 3 to 4 million Germans would drive their own cars.

"Venetien blinds" for rear visibility doubled as engine intake louvers in the 1936 VW prototype (WW3), shown on the right, and the 1937 prototype (VW30), left. A window, not visible from the outside, separated the passenger and engine compartments.

Porsche traveled to the United States in 1936 to visit the Detroit auto plants. While he was away, three prototype Volksautos, as they were now being called, were subjected to grueling road tests, running 400 miles a day, six days a week. As the cars broke down, they were towed in, fixed, and sent back out on the road.

By the 1937 Auto Show, Hitler was running out of patience; four years had passed and he still didn't have his car. He challenged the RDA, and in response they requested a 200-mark subsidy for each car built. Hitler reasoned at that price, he could build his own factory and make the car himself.

In May 1937, The Volkswagen Development Corporation was formed by the state and financed with 480,000 marks from the German Labor Front. (The financing was later increased to 150 million marks.) The company produced thirty more test vehicles. The cars were test-driven for 1½ million miles all over Germany by experienced drivers, most of whom were SS. Flaws, kinks, and weak points were hammered out. Another thirty cars were produced and each was driven for 50,000 miles. At the end of the rigors, Hitler had

the car with the familiar flush headlights and full-length hood, the Type 38. He was now ready for production.

The Fuhrer dangled the car before the German people. Like a barker, he promoted it at the impossible price of 990 marks. Not mentioned was the extra 250 marks for insurance and delivery, even though buyers had to pick up their car at the factory. The fine print was also vague about delivery dates.

Few Germans had the money to buy the car—the cost was equal to about 800 working hours—so a savings plan was instituted using stamp books. Savings-plan participants went to their neighborhood Nazi Party office every week and

The V1, with rear-hinged doors, was one of the first three prototypes tested in 1936. The tests were a lesson in what could go wrong with a car.

Right: Bombing raids over Wolfsburg in 1944 destroyed about 60 percent of the factory. Cars were made at the rate of a few a day, mostly for the Allied occupying forces. One such car is visible in the lower right of the photo. *Below:* VWs coming off the assembly line at Wolfsburg.

purchased a stamp that cost five marks (about two dollars). When the requisite five books were filled, a saver received a certificate of ownership—but not a car. The minimum was later reduced to five marks a month, which made the plan easier on the pocketbook, but rather hopeless in terms of ever saving the prescribed amount. At the rate of five marks a week, it would take four years and seven months to become eligible for a car; at five marks a month, about sixteen years. Those who signed up for the program were legally bound to a non-cancellable, non-transferrable contract.

Some historians, including William L. Shirer, author of *The Third Reich: A History of Nazi Germany* (New York: Fawcett Books, 1991), claim that Hitler intended to use the stamp-program money to build a factory that would make war vehicles. But most agree that he was serious about building his car. As proof of this, $67 million marks belonging to the savers was still in the KdF account at the end of the war. The money was seized by the Soviet Union and never returned.

It is true, however, that while Hitler now had his car, he still needed a factory. The site chosen was a mosquito-infested swamp in a town in Lower Saxony called Fallersleben. On May 26, 1938, Hitler laid the cornerstone for the new factory with banners flying. About 70,000 people attended the cere-

mony, during which Hitler took Porsche by surprise with the announcement that the car would go forth into the world with the name KdF-Wagen, or the "Strength-through-Joy" car. Although promotional materials used the name KdF-Wagen, the general public continued to refer to it as the Volkswagen—even the factory was called the Volkswagenwerk. After the ceremony, Hitler was driven off in a KdF-Wagen to the Fallersleben railway station—back to his war.

Hitler had already invaded and annexed Austria; war plans were escalating and shortages of workers and materials inhibited the building of the Volkswagenwerk and the surrounding town. In September 1939, Hitler invaded Poland and World War II began, slowing construction even more.

The factory did not produce a single car for a German citizen during the war. Before its construction was even finished, the factory's output was converted to military contracts. Even at that, the plant never came close to full production. Other output included mines and parts for the Ju-88 bomber, and toward the end of the war it assembled V-1 flying bombs as well. It also built 1½ million primitive stoves that were shipped to the Russian front.

As it became clear that cars would no longer be produced through the war, important machinery was moved out of the factory and hidden around Europe. In 1944, the Allies bombed the plant, leaving most of it in rubble. Replacing the hidden machinery would have been impossible, and there would have been no future for a post-war Volkswagen.

In April 1945, a handful of American soldiers occupied the town, which the Allies renamed Wolfsburg. At the end of the war, the plant ended up in the British occupation zone. A few Germans, often knee deep in water, cleaned up the debris and retrieved the hidden machinery. The plant was set up as an official repair location for British vehicles, as workers sought to exchange work for food. The British were trying to create jobs for this war-wrecked nation—and Wolfsburg was crawling with refugees.

As Heinz Nordoff, a German who would soon take over running the plant, commented, "by one of the ironic jokes history is sometimes tempted to produce, it was the Occupation Powers who, after unconditional surrender, brought Hitler's dream into reality." The plant was jerry-rigged into action and by the end of 1945, 6,000 workers had produced 1,785 new Volkswagens. Some of the first post-war vehicles produced in Europe, they were made in a factory with holes in the roof that nobody owned and nobody wanted. Cars were bartered for much needed supplies, including food and other necessities for the workers.

In 1946, the factory turned out the 10,000th Volkswagen. Workers placed signs across its windshield that read: "10,000 cars and nothing in the stomach, who can stand that?" In 1947, production dropped to 8,978.

In 1948, the British made one more attempt to unload the factory, offering it to Henry Ford. His advisors made the legendary comment that the factory was "not worth a damn." At one point there was a plan to level the factory, but the idea was rejected. Heinz Nordoff was put in charge, chosen because of his track record at Adam Opel AG, General Motors in Germany. He was also available and in need of a job. Nordoff didn't have too many warm feelings for the car he was about to produce, but he approached his challenge with a serious commitment. He built up spirit and pride among his workers. He began to build an organization.

The birth of the people's car was fraught with difficulties and rife with politics; it suffocated in war, only to be reborn. At this point in history, it was about to become a legend.

British officers charged with responsibility for the plant right after the war were, unlike almost everyone else, very enthused about the Beetle. They kept production going during the first difficult months. Here, workers and officials celebrate the 1000th Beetle to come off the assembly line.

The **1000th** VOLKSWAGEN built during MARCH 1946 coming from Assembly Line

The Beetle circa 1958, the
year the rear window and
windshield were enlarged.
The price was $1,545.

THE BEETLE GOES GLOBAL

The first decade after the war was vital to the future of Volkswagen. Ownership of the company was turned over to the West German Federal Government by the Allies. Free from the constraints of management and external directors, Heinz Nordoff focused on his obsession with quality and the durability of the car. He concentrated all his efforts on design, manufacturing, and inspection, and resisted extreme pressure to redesign the Volkswagen.

"The only decision I am really proud of is that I have refused to change Porsche's design," he said. "It's hard to remain the same. You can always sell cars by being new. But we chose a different course." Pressure to change the car came from dealers as well as people at the plant. "I brushed away all temptations to change model and design. In any sound design there are almost unlimited possibilities—and this certainly was a sound one. I see no sense in starting anew every few years with the same teething troubles, making obsolete almost all the past...Offering people an honest value, a product of the highest quality, with low original cost and incomparable resale value appealed more to me than being driven around by a bunch of hysterical

What do you call your Beetle? In Germany, it's a Käfer; in Japan, the Kabuto-mushi. It's the Bobla in Norway and the Bublan in Sweden. In Italy, it's the Maggiolino; the Escarabajo in Spain. The French call it the Coccinelle, and in the Philippines, it's the Pagong.

stylists trying to sell people something they really do not want to have…." Instead of constantly remodeling the car, he focused on improving the skittish engine and knocking the kinks out of the car—it was thinking that went against the norm of the auto industry.

Nordoff first attempted to enter the U.S. market in 1949. He wanted to buy American machinery and desperately needed American currency to do so. Unfortunately, the U. S. market was deaf, dumb, and blind to the charms of what was still being referred to as Hitler's car. Yet the reluctance to buy the car was less about Hitler than it was about this ugly little bug trying to establish a place for itself in the era of Detroit's tailfins, V-8 engines, and gaudy chrome. A Dutchman named Ben Pon, who had successfully sold Volkswagens in anti-German Holland, was sent to America to line up distributors. His trip was an utter failure. Not one distributor signed on and he ended up selling the car for $800 to pay for his hotel bill and trip home. A few months later, Nordoff himself came to America to try to sell the car with an equal lack of success.

By 1950, Volkswagens had a real option list, including the folding sun roof and hydraulic brakes for export models. The 100,000th Beetle was produced in 1950 by a labor force that had grown to 13,305. Volkswagen was capturing 41.5 percent of all German car sales. They were also creating a major export program while other German manufacturers were concentrating on domestic sales.

Volswagens went to twenty-nine different countries in 1951. Belgium, Sweden, and Switzerland were their major export markets. The year before, Nordoff finally had hired a distributor in America to establish a beachhead. Max Hoffman was a New York importer and wholesaler who dealt mostly in high-performance cars. He added Volkswagen to his line and "convinced" retailers to take a Volkswagen as part of their order. They took the Beetles to ensure delivery of the other cars, but soon found the VWs disappearing off their lots faster than the Jags and Porsches.

In October 1952, the Volkswagen sported a list of new features including vent windows in the front doors, wide bumpers, and a new dash layout that dropped the small left-hand

Below, left: The split rear window of the early 1950s. Right: Volkswagen public relations never let seriousness get in the way of the car's charm. Here, the company demonstrates the retracting steel roof, with its own special twist.

dash bin in exchange for a driver's side-door pocket. Export models even offered synchromesh on top of three ratios. Volkswagen exported 41.4 percent of all Beetles manufactured that year.

By 1953, Volkswagen's sales in America had risen from an anemic 330 in 1950 to a still-anemic 2,173. Compared to the 6 million cars sold in America in those years, VW wasn't even a blip. While the company exported 70,000 cars all over the world, they barely penetrated the American market. Nordoff dropped Max Hoffman and set out to create a new system for selling Beetles.

He wanted recognizable establishments and a support system for parts and service. "In those days," says Baron Bates, who was with Volkswagen Public Relations from 1961 to 1979, "Renault was the major import car. Renault was in dealerships that primarily sold American cars. So when the Renault owner went to get their car fixed, there might be a mechanic who had some training fixing Renaults, but the parts were in France and had to be shipped over." Nordoff, through his lieutenants, established Volkswagen of America with both Germans and Americans heading the organization. They had complete autonomy from Wolfsburg as long as the cars sold well.

There were fifteen regional distributorships, most owned by men who loved automobiles and understood the Volkswagen. Over 1,000 dealerships were established, with dealers hand-picked based on a set of criteria that would fit the Volkswagen way: They had plenty of operating experience, adequate capital, were industrious and cheerful. Now a Volkswagen dealership could be recognized by its glass front and blue-and-white VW sign. As the waiting lists of intended buyers grew, so did the wait for a new VW.

LOOK MA, NO RADIATOR!

Volkswagen's 1964 four-cylinder

rear engine generated 40 HP at 3900 r.p.m. Built

with a magnesium crank case and aluminum cyliner heads,

total "dry" weight of the VW-1200 engine was about 220 pounds.

Piston displacement was 1192 cubic centimeters (72.24 cubic inches). The

fan blows 18 cubic of cooling air across the engine every second when the

engine is running at 3600 r.p.m. By 1970, horsepower increased to 57, and

displacement was enlarged to 1600 cc. By comparison, the New Beetle is

powered by a front-mounted, 115 HP four-cylinder engine or, as an

option, a highly advanced Turbo Direct Injection diesel that

delivers an estimated EPA rating of 48 mpg on the

highway and 41 in the city.

OFFICIAL CAR OF THE REVOLUTION

It is no accident that Volkswagen started advertising seriously when Carl Hahn was sent to America to enlarge the dealership network and strengthen the organizational structure. Volkswagen was preparing in all possible ways for Detroit's compact-car counter-attack against the growing market share claimed by foreign vehicles. In model year 1960, the Valiant, Falcon, and Corvair were to arrive and compete with the Beetle.

Hahn was a detail man. He appreciated statistics, analysis, and the information one could gain from data. His advertising manager, Helmut Schmitz, was also an analytical person. Together they simply sought out an advertising agency that they felt could handle this very different car.

Auto advertising in 1959 was all the same. It has been described by those who were there as mediocre, safe, and often created by committee. Ads were illustrated, never photographed, which allowed the agencies to elongate and glamorize the cars with glittering starbursts bouncing off the chrome that adorned the automobiles of the time. There was no need to worry about accuracy in the copy since the ads were virtually fact-free. The space was filled with models in enviable settings looking glamorous, healthy, and wealthy.

How many students can you fit in a Beetle? The record was apparently set at Bournemouth College of Technology and College of Art, where 103 students packed themselves in and still managed to drive the car fifteen feet.

Below: A 1962 model of the most popular convertible ever built, the Cabriolet. *Bottom right:* The VW "lollipop" logo identifies the original Volkswagen of America headquarters, built in 1964 in New Jersey.

tire in the water with regional newspaper advertising that seemed to help recognition, but the dealer network was ready for national advertising.

The challenge was to find an agency that didn't produce advertising *du jour*. Intrigued by the work Doyle Dane Bernbach had done for other clients, they met. Hahn liked David Bernbach's honesty and wit—and he liked the fact that the agency's people stood up to them and defended their creative. DDB got the account and an $800,000 budget. Despite the small budget (in its first four months, Edsel's agency spent $8 million), the account was as good for DDB as it was for Volkswagen.

Thirty years have passed and the campaign produced by DDB for Volkswagen is still often referred to as the best advertising ever done for a consumer product. Hahn's advertising

Why Volkswagen even wanted to advertise since there was a six-month waiting period for the car is another story. Put in his own serviceable English, Schmitz said, "We wanted to start to advertise not because we were in trouble but because we wanted to avoid to get in trouble." Word-of-mouth was selling 150,000 cars a year and the company felt that a saturation point had been reached. Volkswagen put one

'49	'50	'51	'52	'53	'54	'55	'56	'57	'58	'59	'60	'61	'62	'63	'64	'65	'66	'67	'68	'69	'70	'71	'72	'73	'74	'75	'76	'77	'78	'79	'80	'81

430,000
400,000

300,000

200,000

100,000

The Retail Sales History of the Volkswagen Beetle in America (Source: VWOA)

The 1969 Beetle was ever-popular with the campus crowd. This model offered an automatic stick shift converter transmission that eliminated the clutch pedal, which made gear-changing in traffic unnecessary, but still permitted shifting. *Far Left:* The Beetle's infallibility was always being tested in interesting ways.

manager spoke of the ads this way, "The very style of our ads gives the impression already of utter simplicity. Of direct-ness. Of honesty. It is not Disneyland that people are looking at in our ads. Not a dream world. Not never-never land. It's reality. We just show a car. Sometimes with people. But with real people. Sometimes in a situation. But a real situation."

The first thing the DDB team did when they got the account was go to Wolfsburg and spend days talking to everyone at the factory—engineers, executives, assembly workers. They walked through the entire process of making the Beetle and witnessed the final moment as it drove off the assembly line. That experience at the factory proved invalu-able. It told them what to say about the car, told them what the customer would want to know: the quality of the materi-als, the care taken in making the car, the unbelievable inspec-tion process, and the efficiency of the operation that resulted in low cost for the consumer.

There were guidelines for VW advertising. They never knocked the competition. They never lied or exaggerated. They were always honest and humorous. They took a person-to-person approach that was often self-deprecating. They followed these rules religiously. And they took many risks, some of which were questioned in Wolfsburg. Perhaps the two most controversial ads produced and run by DDB were entitled, "Lemon" and "We don't have anything to show you in our new models." The first just flew in the face of convention. There was no precedent, no reason to conclude that running an ad with the headline "Lemon" below your product was a good idea. It must have taken a gigantic leap of faith for the Germans to approve such an idea. The second headline ran under a blank space. The company was upset at running a blank space that cost so much. Dealers reported that this ad brought in more inquiries than any previous ad and Wolfsburg changed its tune.

In 1960, foreign cars represented 10 percent of the total sales of automobiles in the United States. The Beetle, bolstered by DDB advertising, surprised the American

auto world by capturing the hearts, minds, and pocketbooks of an entire generation. "The car was certainly not produced as anything but a peoples' car," says Art Railton who was the public relations chief at Volkswagen in its heyday. "It was thought of as a well-made piece of machinery that the average man could own. It was totally unexpected that it would cross all class lines. But no where in the [sales] equation was the fact that this car was fun to drive, fun to look at, and fun to talk about."

Left: The 1966 Volkswagen family still starred the Beetle, but added several other models. Clockwise from the Beetle is the Squareback, the Stationwagon or "Bus," the Karmann Ghia, and the Fastback. *Below:* An early cabriolet. *Right:* A small sampling of the all-time classic advertising campaign created by Doyle Dane Bernbach.

Lemon.

This Volkswagen missed the boat.

The chrome strip on the glove compartment is blemished and must be replaced. Chances are you wouldn't have noticed it; Inspector Kurt Kroner did.

There are 3,389 men at our Wolfsburg factory with only one job: to inspect Volkswagens at each stage of production. (3000 Volkswagens are produced daily; there are more inspectors than cars.)

Every shock absorber is tested (spot checking won't do), every windshield is scanned. VWs have been rejected for surface scratches barely visible to the eye.

Final inspection is really something! VW inspectors run each car off the line onto the Funktionsprüfstand (car test stand), tote up 189 check points, gun ahead to the automatic brake stand, and say "no" to one VW out of fifty.

This preoccupation with detail means the VW lasts longer and requires less maintenance, by and large, than other cars. (It also means a used VW depreciates less than any other car.)

We pluck the lemons; you get the plums.

How much longer can we hand you this line?

Forever, we hope.

Because nobody ever intends to change the Volkswagen's shape.

The only reason the Volkswagen is ever changed is to make it work even better.

The money that isn't spent on outside changes is spent inside the car.

This system provides an immense advantage: Time. Years of it.

There's time to improve parts and still keep most of them interchangeable.

(Which is why it's so easy to get VW parts, and why our mechanics don't wake up screaming.)

There's time to put an immense amount of hand work into each VW, and to finish each one like a $16,000 machine.

And this system has also kept the price of the Volkswagen almost the same over the years.

Some cars keep changing and stay the same.

Volkswagens stay the same and keep changing.

Think small.

Our little car isn't so much of a novelty any more.

A couple of dozen college kids don't try to squeeze inside it.

The guy at the gas station doesn't ask where the gas goes.

Nobody even stares at our shape.

In fact, some people who drive our little flivver don't even think 32 miles to the gallon is going any great guns.

Or using five pints of oil instead of five quarts.

Or never needing anti-freeze.

Or racking up 40,000 miles on a set of tires.

That's because once you get used to some of our economies, you don't even think about them any more.

Except when you squeeze into a small parking spot. Or renew your small insurance. Or pay a small repair bill. Or trade in your old VW for a new one.

Think it over.

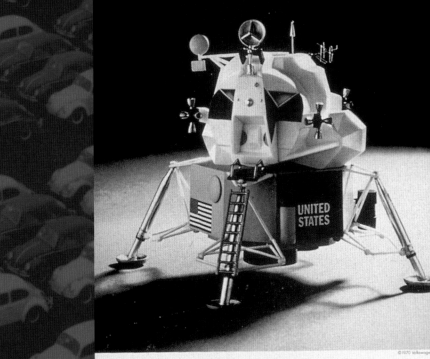

It's ugly, but it gets you there.

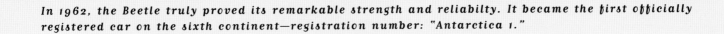

In 1962, the Beetle truly proved its remarkable strength and reliabilty. It became the first officially registered car on the sixth continent—registration number: "Antarctica 1."

This little Beetle, the sales of which more than tripled in five years, became more than a car. The Beetle and its first cousin, the Bus, were the official cars of the revolution. But there was more. There was Beetle stuffing—trying to break the record for the number of people put into the car at one time. There were sexual triumphs in a cubby-hole sized space. There were custom paint jobs like never before. The bug became a caricature of itself with bug eyes and beetle wings as well as a canvas for the self-expression of psyche-delic artists. There were kits that let you make your Beetle into a Rolls Royce. There were freelance alterations too, like those who made their Beetles into a horse-drawn carriage or a covered wagon. The Beetle floated—and the floating cre-

ated a whole subculture. The Waterbugs of America Racing Association events required participants to enter the water at speed and negotiate a water course of about a mile. There were the inevitable attempts to cross the English Channel floating in a VW.

In the 1960s, everything changed. The dominant forces moved society from the basic black of the beat generation to wild psychedelic colors of the LSD generation. Jazz was replaced by The Beatles, the Rolling Stones, and the Grateful Dead. What was it about Volkswagen's appeal that allowed the company to sell every car they shipped to America? Did it have anything to do with the changes that were going on—or would this car have become an icon at any time in American history?

It's not an easy question to answer, but one wants to believe that this people's car, this little unassuming, cute, cheap, functioning car fit the ideas and the cultural leanings of the time.

"The key to Volkswagen's success is simple," said Carl

Opposite: Although many a car-chase has eclipsed an actor's role, no car has had a more stellar movie career than the Beetle. At top, a scene from *The Love Bug Rides Again,* one of three sequels to the 1969 Walt Disney movie *The Love Bug,* starring Herbie, the Volkswagen with a heart. Below, hon-eymooners Ken Berry and Stephanie Powers ride Herbie under a wedding arch of VWs. Other notable screen appear-ances include Annie Hall's fashionable gold bug, as well as supporting per-formances in *What's Up, Doc?* and *Forrest Gump.* *Left:* The most popular car in the world, 1969.

Hahn in 1961. "An honest product aimed at satisfying a basic consumer need will always sell. This universal truth…is our secret." The car simply became "in." Says Railton, "Public relations and advertising had little to do with its success.…When they started advertising, there were only a limited number of cars coming to America and the demand was greater than the number of cars so the sales couldn't have

ed a 55 percent share of imported cars and a 5.5 share of all automobiles sold that year. In 1969, there was a stagnation of the auto market, a dock strike that kept VWs out of the U.S. market, and a devaluation of the German mark that forced VW to raise its prices. Volkswagen still sold cars in 1969 and produced the 4 millionth VW for America. But

gone up anymore. But the advertising made it more loveable and gave it more personality."

The record year for VW sales (all cars) in the U.S. was 1968, when they sold 569,292 Volkswagens. That represent-

the company was branching out, making many different kinds of vehicles: station wagons, fast backs, and buses, as well as Beetles. And now they had Audis and Porsches to sell as well.

4

THE DECLINE
AND FALL

The Beetle became increasingly sophisticated technically after 1968, but America was changing. The Beetle and Volkswagen were no longer on the must-be-seen-driving list.

The Japanese were building better small cars and the Beetle's design was seen as old hat as customers gravitated to Hondas, Toyotas, and American-made compact cars. Volkswagen introduced a bare-bones model that cost $1,845, yet new circumstances were causing sales to crash. Their introduction of the Super Beetle moved the needle for Volkswagen. The Super Beetle had a redesigned engine, a trunk with more space, MacPherson struts that improved front suspension, and a rated top speed of 83 mph. Price: $2,299.

Although the 1970s was a period of decline for Volkswagen in America, the decade was not without its high points. On February 15, 1972, the Beetle passed the Ford Model T's production at 15,007,034, making it the most produced automobile in history.

Despite the higher sticker prices due in part to a strong Deutchmark, VW sold more than 476,000 vehicles in the U.S. in 1973, partly because of the Super Beetle. In 1974, the fuel crisis squeezed even the Beetle. Sales declined to just over 240,000 units, a drop of 120,000. The company insisted that they would keep making the Beetle as long as there was a demand, but in fact they stopped making the Beetle at Wolfsburg in July of 1974. In its place they began producing the Golf and the Rabbit. Although

The 1970 sedan featured a slightly larger engine that gave it great response and more rapid acceleration in the lower ranges of its four-speed synchromesh transmission.

assembly did continue in Europe, the Beetle's production continued to drop. In 1978, production of the Beetle was transferred to Puebla, Mexico.

Beetles continued to be sold in the U.S. from 1975 to 1977. La Grande Bug, the last Super Beetle sedan, brought the Beetle's cachet to a new high. Nonetheless, 1975 was the last year for the Super Beetle. All Beetle sedans built after 1975 went back to Porsche's original chassis layout. But front-drive, water-cooled Volkswagen models were competing with the

Beetle and the car simply wasn't high-tech enough for most customers. In 1977, the Beetle gave up in America. Sales had plummeted from 90,000 in 1975 to less than 20,000 in just three years. The last German Beetle was completed on January 19, 1978.

Only the Beetle cabriolet convertible remained in production and actually maintained its popularity until it was replaced by the Karmann-built Rabbit convertible in 1980. The idea to build a cabriolet version of the Beetle began after the war. A famous coachbuilder, Wilhelm Karmann approached the Wolfsburg factory and asked to acquire a chassis .upon which he could build a

cabriolet. Since Wolfsburg was the only auto plant functioning after the was, it was vital to Karmann's business to get a chassis. After several refusals, he was given the 10,000th postwar-built Beetle.

Soon two prototype Volkswagen cabriolets were built at the Karmann factory in Osnabruck, Germany. Removing the roof of the Beetle caused the car to lose rigidity. Karmann strengthened the body shell, adding more weight. After as many as twenty-five pre-production models, the car passed muster with Volkswagen.

Production was slow to start, and over the course of the next thirty years, only 331, 847 cabriolets were built—just over 10,000 a year. Production ended on January 10, 1980. The last two to be made were all-white; one of them now resides at the Karmann factory museum in Osnabruck.It had a good run of thirty-one years, producing 332,000 cars, making it the most popular open car ever made.

On May 15, 1981, VW celebrated the 20 millionth Beetle. It came off the line at Puebla, Mexico, with a Silver Bug designation and a matching key fob. There were still a few new features to be added in terms of Mexican production: a new electric windshield washer pump in 1982, for instance. And VW marketed "special" series to its audience of Beetle devotees.

At various times between 1945 and 1984, Beetles, including convertibles, were built in five different German factories, in addition to construction or assembly that took place in nineteen other countries from Uruguay to Ireland, New Zealand to Brazil. The original Beetle is still manufactured in Mexico today.

Those who love the Beetle have imbued it with all kinds of attributes that take the simple car far beyond its everyday mission—and most of the time, it doesn't disappoint. Walter Henry Nelson refers to stories in the

When Volkswagen stopped selling Beetles in America, they inadvertently created one of the auto industry's healthiest second-hand markets. As scenes from the 1988 VW collectors' rally in Fremont, California, show, Beetle owners continued to parade their colors.

Volkswagen customer magazine, *Small World*, about airplanes using Volkswagen engines.

Converting Beetles actually became a big business for one company, first called European Motor Products, Inc., then Engineered Motor Products, Inc. (EMPI). EMPI was the brainchild of VW dealer Joe Vittone, who went to various manufacturers for engine converters and sold items like the anti-roll bar that helped the Beetle handle like a sports car and the stabilizer bar or camber compensator that stopped the back wheels from tucking under during hard cornering.

VWs continue to be used in competition and endurance racing with great success. When it first entered competitions with racing cars twice its power and twice the price, onlookers were amused. Amusement quickly turned to awe as the Beetle wins began to mount.

9

10

A BEETLE IS A BEETLE IS A BEETLE, RIGHT?

Not if you look closely enough. Each year, Volkswagen introduced a number of alterations and improvements. Clockwise from the top of the opposite page: (1) In 1951, the Beetle featured the original split rear window with single tail and brake lights. (2) For 1952, vent windows are added. (3) A one-piece rear window replaces the split window on March 10, 1953. (4) Bumper overrider bows are added. (5) Front turn-signal lights moved to the top of the fenders in 1959, and the rear window and windshield were enlarged. (6) In 1962, larger

7

6

taillights are added. (7) A crank-operated sliding steel sunroof

replaces the fabric sunroof in 1964. (8) In 1968, one-piece bumpers are intro-

duced, the bows and overrides are eliminted (raising the bumper height), and

back-up brake lights and rear turn signals are contained in a single housing.

(9) The 1973 model has larger circular taillight complex that combines stoplight,

turn signal, tail, and backup lights. (10) The bustled skirt was added below

the rear bumper in 1975.

THE NEW BEETLE

When Volkswagen unveiled their Concept 1 vehicle at the 1994 Detroit Auto Show, they weren't prepared for the reaction. Concept cars always get a lot of attention, but they rarely make it to the showrooms. And yet everyone who saw Concept 1 said, "Are you going to make this car? Build it. Build it." Volkswagen didn't get serious about building it right then and there, but they were overwhelmed by the reaction. It was what they had been looking for—a way to get back the loyal customers who had moved on.

Volkswagen hit the skids in America, selling only 49,000 Volkswagen models and 12,000 Audis in 1994. Out of this desperation came the idea for the New Beetle. Volkswagen's California Design Studio, headed at the time by Freeman Thomas and J. Mays (who later became chief designer at Ford), felt that the logical way for Volkswagen to get its customers back was through its most successful car—the Beetle. The key words the team wrote on the blackboard when designing the car were "honest, simple, reliable, and emotional." The inspirational motto seems to have worked.

Visually, much of the New Beetle is based on the circle. Says one of the members of the design team for Concept 1, "We spent a lot of time throwing cardboard shapes onto the conference table and moving them around. The circle won every time. It is the most pleasing shape."

The universal recognition of the original Beetle often led to its use as a standard of measure—even by the U.S. military. For example: "The 16-inch guns of the U.S.S. New Jersey can, in effect, hurl a Volkswagen with enough force to penetrate 30 feet of reinforced concrete."

The New Beetle arrived in March 1998, amid great excitement. Would it sell? Would it be a success? Isn't it cute? It isn't the old Beetle, but people seem to love it just the same. With so much talk and so much speculation, it's the most exciting introduction since the Ford Mustang in 1964.

At $15,200, plus a $500 destination charge, the New Beetle is 36 percent more expensive than a 1977 Beetle would be in 1998 dollars.

The details make the New Beetle look custom-made. Headlights and taillights sit directly into the body. The round headlights house the projector-beam halogen headlamp as well as the turn signals and daytime running lights. Fenders, made of dent-resistant plastic, are the color of the car. There is no chrome as there was on the old Beetle. The trunk lock, cleverly disguised behind a round VW logo, swivels to the side to reveal an integrated handle that helps raise the hatch back. Inside there is room—10.3 cubic feet of it—for stowage. The underside of the hatch has grab indentations that make it easier to close.

Circles are everywhere. Circles inside circles as you look at the brushed aluminum wheel covers. The fat circular steering wheel is made of industrial brushed aluminum and

rubber. The instrument gauge is a circle that displays the speed, rev counter, engine temperature, and fuel gauge. It does recall the old Beetle's round speedometer set in front of the old, thin, round steering wheel. On the dash are vents—circular in shape. The circles are made out of beautiful, tactile materials—an antidote to the boring black-on-white Teutonic interiors that are today's norm.

Wolfsburg was divided about building the New Beetle. The anti-Beetle camp thought they should build a more rational car for America. The pro-Beetle camp thought that America had enough rational cars and that they needed to get Americans emotional about Volkswagen again. "It took us about nine months to get the project far enough through the system to build a model," said one designer. "We built one and presented it to Ferdinand Piech, the grandson of Ferdinand Porsche, who now heads Volkswagen, in a twenty-five-minute meeting. "He just smiled," remembered one team member. "It was a nice moment." And then Piech said, "Build it."

It still took a lot of doing. There were conflicts over the size of the car. The designers wanted to build the Beetle on the Polo platform or understructure. Ultimately it was built on the Golf

Left: **The Concept 1 was the show car at the 1994 Auto Show in Detroit.** *Opposite, clockwise from top:* **The Concept 1 Cabriolet. Enthusiasts wax poetic over the New Beetle's headlights; like the taillights, they are set into the body of the car. The New Beetle has a smile for everyone.**

The Beetle steering wheel of 1962, with its characteristic Wolfsburg logo, as compared with that of the new. Elements of the old Beetle are reinterpreted and the circle motif is played to the fullest. The blue indigo of the display and the red indicator needles are primary. It's simple, playful, and employs high-quality textured plastics and textiles.

platform, which is larger than the Polo, because it met all the requirements for the American market. The designers still feel that the Beetle is too big—by about five or six inches—but that hasn't stopped the public from buying every New Beetle that gets built.

The New Beetle takes off at a *brrmm, brrmm hum*. The standard 5-speed manual gearbox and its 2.0 liter/115 horsepower, single overhead cam (SOHC) engine feels good. If you are thinking about your old Beetle circa 1970, which had 57 horsepower, the pick-up is surprising.

Like its forebear, the New Beetle has four-wheel independent suspension. The front has MacPherson struts with control arms, stabilizer bar, and coil spring struts. The rear has a V-profile independent torsion beam axle with integral sway bar and trailing arms—all of which amounts to good engineering stuff that gives you a smooth ride and a solid feeling around corners.

The New Beetle is larger than the original. It is 67.9 inches wide, 161.1 inches long and 59.5 inches high, and rides on a 98.9 wheelbase. *Road & Track* magazine compared the new dimensions with a 1967 1500 cc sedan that measured 160.6 inches long, rode on a 94.5-inch wheelbase, and weighed 1790 pounds—almost a half-ton lighter than the New Beetle.

To be able to buy a car for $15,000 that makes you feel special is an amazing feat (and ironic when you consider that an old Beetle cost as little as $1,500). The published price when the Beetle was born in 1998 for the 2.0 liter gasoline engined-car was $15,200 and $16,475 for the Turbo Direct Injection (TDI). Of course, since the car was selling out, dealers could sell to the highest bidder.

Made exclusively in Volkswagen's Puebla, Mexico, plant, the company projected producing 130,000 vehicles the first year. Fifty-thousand were slated for America and another 8,000 for Canada. VW sales rose 50 percent to 104,081 cars in the first half of 1998 as Americans rushed to buy the first Beetle since 1977. Europeans clamored for the Beetle, even at a considerably higher price tag of over $19,000, which covered the cost of some features that were standard in Europe but not in America. Volkswagen stated that there were 100,000 Germans who had expressed interest in buying the car, lead-

The more things change, the more they stay the same. *Opposite:* **Volkswagen continues its tradition of showing the substance beneath the style, with their traditional schematic diagrams.** *Above:* **Same engine shot, too—but this time it's in the front of the car.**

LESS FLOWER. MORE POWER.

Suddenly the world's glass is half-full again. 0—60? Yes. Lime. Beetle 2.0. Digitally remastered. Reverse engineered from UFOs. Do these slogans have a familiar ring? The new ad campaign for the New Beetle has a new agency behind it, The Arnold Agency of Boston, but there it is again. The simplicity. The cleverness. The nod to nostalgia. The salute to the new age. Like the old campaign, the name is not used. Says Ron Lawner, managing partner and chief creative officer at Arnold, "What else can it be? It doesn't look like a Buick." Once again, the Beetle has given automotive advertising a fresh, fun face. It is a blessed relief from the rugged outdoor scenes that have become de rigeur with four-wheel drive. This VW campaign is honest, direct, and makes you smile—just like the car. The New Beetle might not need such clever advertising, since Volkswagen can't keep up with the demand, but it helps us love the car even more.

A car like this comes around only twice in a lifetime.

Drivers wanted.

If you sold your soul in the 80s, here's your chance to buy it back.

Drivers wanted.

ing to a gray market of cars being imported to Germany from Mexico and resold to antsy owners.

In addition to its charm, the car has safety features and devices that cannot be compared to the old Beetle because they didn't even exist then. The seats are better, there are front air bags and side air bags that are built right into the seat allowing the airbag to stay with the seat position in case of a crash. There's a more powerful engine, and a new seat belt tensioning system that tightens and optimally positions the front belts within milliseconds of a severe crash. In addition, the body structure of the New Beetle is exceptionally rigid and incorporates energy-absorbing crumple zones that fold like an accordian in a crash. This helps to keep the central structure in place. There's also a collapsible steering column.

Does the New Beetle have staying power? Some say it's a fad. Most say it's a real car,

with real value, and that it has legs. All ages love the car. As Bob Garfield of *Advertising Age* writes, "Everybody will love the New Beetle. Boomers. Teenagers. Amish. Everybody. For one thing, this vehicle will instantaneously replace the VW Cabrio as the official car of Courtney. And Jennifer, and Brittani, and Caitlin, and every other 22-year-old, like, blonde. They won't appreciate the miracle of a working defroster, but their devotion will be unending, nonetheless. They will buy it, cherish it, and in all probability, pierce it."

The comparatively plush front seat of the New Beetle.

CLUBS AND ORGANIZATIONS

Volkswagen clubs and collector associations dedicated to the Beetle—old and new—abound across the United States and around the world. A small sampling is offered here; for a comprehensive international listing, look to the internet at http://www.unaids.org/kabrioletts/club/index.html for the "Exclusively Käfer Kabrioletts" website.

United States

The Official VW Owner's Club
P.O. Box 2012
Bloomfield, MI 48303
(800) 374-8389
Website: http://www.vw.com/vwworld/vwclub

Vintage Volkswagen Club of America (VVWA)
c/o Newsletter
P.O. Box 12443
Overland Park, KS 66282-2443
(Chapters in Arizona, Arkansas, California, Connecticut, Delaware, Florida, Georgia, Illinois, Kansas, Kentucky, Louisiana, Maryland, Michigan, Minnesota, Missouri, Montana, Nebraska, New Hampshire, New Jersey, New York, North Carolina, Ohio, Oregon, Oklahoma, Pennsylvania, South Carolina, Texas, Vermont, Virginia, Washington, Wisconsin.)

Volkswagen Club of America
c/o Newsletter
1554 Roanoke Avenue
Aurora, IL 60506

German Deception-Alaska
16403 Home Place #21
Eagle River, AK 99577

Old Volkswagens of Alabama (OVAL)
1248 Noremac Road
Montgomery, AL 36119
Website: www.sociology.auburn.edu/vw/oval/main/main.html

The Tucson Volkswagen Club
Loren R. Knapp
1002 W. Thurber Street
Tucson, AZ 85705

Capitol City Euros
Sacramento, CA
(916) 321-0163 (Club Hotline)

Vintage Volks of San Diego
7426 Rock Canyon Drive
San Diego, CA 92126
(619) 578-1189

Volkswagen Enthusiasts of Colorado
5164 West Columbia Place
Denver, CO 80236

The Connecticut Volkswagen Association
P.O. Box 4064
Waterbury CT 06704

Common Gear Newsletter
c/o House of Buggin'
P.O. Box 3353
Stony Creek, CT 06405

Delaware Volkswagen Association (South)
100 Sypherd Drive
Newark, DE 19711

Bad Bug Club
16016 U.S. Highway 301
Dade City, FL 33525

Central Florida VW Club
P.O. Box 574921
Orlando, FL 32857-4921

North Georgia VW Club
P.O. Box 53
Homer, GA 30547

Middle Georgia VW Club
104 McKinley Drive
Griffin, GA 30223

Klassich Kruzers of Hawaii
P.O. Box 1021
Kanohe, HI 96744

Der Donner Kafers
1226 14th Street
Lewiston, ID 83501

Chicago Volkswagen Organization, Inc.
P.O. Box 582
LaGrange, IL 60525

Central Indiana Volks Folks
3848 S. Sherman
Indianapolis, IN 46237

The Mid-Iowa VW Association
711 Bancroft Street, #5
Des Moines, IA 50315

The Volkswagen Klub of Kansas
P.O. Box 47371
Wichita, KS 67201

Southern Kentucky Volkswagen Club
P.O. Box 50146
Bowling Green, KY 42102
Website: http://www.premiernet.net/~skvwclub

Crescent City Air Coolers
P.O. Box 764
Metaire, LA 70004

Vacationland VW Association
c/o Jordans Foreign Auto
P.O. Box 16
West Poland, ME 04291

The Maryland Bugweisers
118 Bush Chapel Road
Aberdeen, MD 21001

Bay State Bug Club
P.O. Box 304
Norfolk, MA 02056

Michigan Vintage Volkswagen Club
24600 Rockford
Dearborn, MI 48124-2749
Website: http://members.aol.com/bugguy66/mvvc.html

Gulf Coast Volkswagen Club
15968 Albany Drive
Bilozi, MS 39532

General Registry of Ozarks' Volkswagen Enthusiasts (GROOVE)
c/o Bob Hufford
1825 E. Arlington Drive
Springfield, MO 65803

Missouri Volks Folks
3756 Arcadia
Saint Charles, MO 63301

Volkswagen Club of Nebraska
5736 Ofoe
Lincoln, NE 68506
(402) 475-9939
Website: http://www.ben.esu6.k12.ne.us/ite/vw

Foreign Four VW Club
330 Southern Decatur #330
Las Vegas, NV 89107

New Hampshire Volkswagen Club
P.O. Box 1215
Manchester, NH 03105

Air-Cooled Engine of Greater Mercer County
c/o Luis Vega, President
714 Second Street
Trenton, NJ 08611

Route 66 Split
Cletus Riedel
P.O. Box 695
Cedar Crest, NM 87008

Fingerlakes Region VW Club, Inc.
c/o Joyce Crispino
388 Longbush Lane
Webster, NY 14580

Hudson and Mohawk Society of VW Owners (HAMS)
c/o Scott Lavigne
4 Raymond Lane
Clifton Park, NY 12065

Appalachian Split Screens
c/o Neil Pickett
38 Center Street
Candler, NC 28715

Central Ohio Vintage Volkswagen Club
P.O. Box 82077
Columbus, OH 43202

German Air Sucker Society (GASS)
454 N. Lincoln Avenue
Salem, OH 44460

Mid-America VW Society
P.O. Box 5132
Enid, OK 73702

Good Times VW Club, Inc.
P.O. Box 23141
Eurgen, OR 97402

Three River VW Club
340 Elizabeth Avenue
Pittsburgh, PA 15202

V-Dub Club of Rhode Island
117 Festival Field Apts.
Newport, RI 02815

Palmeto VW Club
520 State Street
West Columbia, SC 29169

Club Vee Dub of East Tennessee
P.O. Box 5646
Knoxville, TN 37918

ARK-LA-TEX VW Club
1507 New Boston Road
Texarkana, TX 75501

Houston Volkswagen Club
P.O. Box 770417
Houston, TX 77215-0417
Website: http://www.autographica.com/hvwc.html

Salt Lake City Air Coolers
914 West 4800 South
Salt Lake City, UT 84123

Valley Air Coolers
Route 2, Box 316-A
Strasburg, VA 22657
(703) 465-4646

Volkswagen Club of Tidewater
P.O. Box 61011
3048 Clastonbury Drive
Virginia Beach, VA 23462

FarFromSlo Volkswagen Club
1239 River Road
Longview, WA 98632-3216
(360) 425-7232
Website: http://www.teleport.com/~vwbug

Milwaukee Area Volkswagen Club
1408 N. 63rd Street
Wauwatosa, WI 53213

Canada

Club Coccinelle de Quebec
863, Mgr Grandin app 8
Sainte-Foy, Quebec G1V3X8

Club Vee Dub Volkswagen Enthusiasts-Calgary
P.O. Box 32058
Bank View Postal Outlet
Calgary, Alberta T2T 5X6

The Ottawa Volkswagen Club
Capital City Volkswagen Association (CCVA)
c/o Ron Cashman
605 Wavell Avenue
Ottawa, Ontario K2A 3A7
(613) 728-2796

Thunderbugs of British Columbia
15060 108th Street
Surrey, British Columbia V3R 1W4

International

International Volkswagen Association (I.V.W.A.)
P.O. Box 25123
Winston-Salem, NC 27114-5123
Website: http://www.ivwa.com

The London and Thames Valley VW Owners Club
John Daniel, LTV
66 Pinewood Green, Iver Heath
Bucks SL0 0QH England
(01753) 651538

Club VeeDub Sydney
P.O. Box 1135
Parramatta NSW 2124
Australia
(02) 9724 4660
Website: http://www.clubvw.org.au

VW Club Incorporated
GPO Box 1215 K
Melbourne 3001
Australia

VW Owners Club
Frank Pronk
P.O. Box 12538
Penrose, Auckland
New Zealand

Volkswagen Owners Club KdF of Japan
#3 Atsushi Nobusawa
KdF Home Page
E-mail: 3s@kakaa.or.jp

PHOTO CREDITS

All of the photographs contained in the book are courtesy Volkswagen of America, except for those appearing on pages 6 (top left and right, and bottom); 24 (bottom); 26 (top and bottom); 27; 36 (bottom left); 38 (top); and 48–49 (all), which were taken by Michael J. Epstein and used with his kind permission.

GUINNESS
RECORD
BREAKERS

TRY THIS!

Robert Wadlow stood 8 feet 11.1 inches tall. How does your hand compare to his?

GUINNESS
RECORD
BREAKERS

KAREN ROMANO YOUNG

GUINNESS MEDIA, INC.

CONTENTS

Are you a Guinness Record Breaker?

Being a Guinness Record Breaker is about doing what you do well and what you love – whatever that is. It's about doing your best, and, sometimes, doing it better than anyone else. We hope this book inspires you to learn more about the world and about yourself and what you're good at. And if you want to set a record along the way, let us know before you start. To begin, turn the page.

The Record-Breaker for Breaking Records

You can make 'em, you can break 'em. They're records, and Ashrita Furman has more than anyone else. Here, he tells you how.

> "I truly believe that every single person has some talent that he or she could develop to the point of saying, 'I'm the best in the world.'"

Most Records

Ashrita Furman, of New York, N.Y., has held the most records: 47, and counting. Some have been broken, but many still stand. You can check out all his records in the chart at right.

How he does it

Ashrita explains how to set a record, step by step.

1. Choose a record. "*The Guinness Book of World Records* says to me, 'You can do anything if you try.' Pick something you might be good at".

2. Get the record guidelines. Every record has its own set of rules. That's how Guinness makes sure that anyone anywhere who tries a record has a fair shot at it. Write to Guinness Media to get the guideline The address is on page 64.

3. Plan your record attempt. Where are you going to set your record? (You might want to try a few places before choosing one.) When will yo do it? (You might need to get permission.) Who will be your timers, judges, helpers? (Guinness is strict about who you use. Be careful!) Check your guidelines and line up everything – and everyone – you'll need. Get an adult to supervise this, so you can concentrate on your training.

4. Get yourself ready. Work out. Work up to what you'll have to do to set your record. And don't get too discouraged if it takes longer than yo think. "The first time I tried to somersault for a distance, I got dizzy and nauseous," says Ashrita. "I said, 'This is impossible!' Then I told myself, 'That guy in the book did it, I can do it, too.' And I did it." Ashrita's advice: " It may not happen as fast as you think – but you'll do it sometime!"

5. All set for the big day: You've got your people, your place, your things – everything the guidelines say you need. Now it's up to you.

6. Go! Going....going...that record's gone! But your work is not done.

7. Let Guinness know. Send in your materials – your video, your photographs, your newspaper stories, your logbook – everything the guidelines told you you'd need to prove your new record.

8. It's official! If you've set a record, Guinness will send you a certificate in the mail. You've done it!

Fastest Speed on Stilts

Ashrita does not hold this record – yet. The record, held by M. Garisoain, is 4.97 miles in 42 minutes. That record has stood since 1892!

Dream Record

The whole time we were working on this book, Ashrita was trying for the stilt-walking record. First he learned how to walk on the stilts. "Lots of falls," says Ashrita. He worked on building up the muscles on the sides of his legs. Then trouble hit. During a visit to Zimbabwe, Ashrita rode a horse through a wildlife park. When he rode too near some giraffes, the horse bucked. Ashrita was thrown, and he tore some muscles. It was several months before he could get back on stilts. He trained, his stilts broke, he trained on new stilts, and he trained some more...and he was still getting ready when we went to press.

Breaking News

Did Ashrita break the stilts record before we went to press? See page 64.

TRY THIS!

Look for Ashrita practicing his records all through this book. How many Ashritas can you find? (Answer: page 64.)

Milk Bottle Balancing

Ashrita's longest milk balancing walk was 83 miles.

How he does it

"The milk bottle record is my trademark. It was set by a clown in 1981, and I broke it in 1983. It's been a part of my life ever since." Others have broken Ashrita's milk bottle record, but he always tries to win it back – six times, in all.

The hardest part of setting the milk bottle record is being patient. First, you have to walk a long way. "It takes so much concentration, but it's totally silly – I love that!"

A Life of Record-Breaking

Records (number broken)	Ashrita's Best Record
Jumping jacks (3)	45,027
Somersaults/distance (2)	12 miles, 390 yards
Somersaults/speed (2)	1 mile / 19 minutes 38 seconds
Hand clapping (1)	50 hours
Stretcher bearing/team (1)	27 miles / 5 hours
Most expensive wreath (1)	10,000 flowers / $3,500
Milk bottle balancing (6)	83 miles
Pogo stick, distance (4)	16 miles
Aqua pogo (underwater) (2) †	3 hours, 40 minutes
Skip running (1) †	10 miles (1 hour, 15 minutes, 33 seconds)
Juggling (1)	6 hours, 7 minutes
Land rowing (2)	1,500 miles
Pogo juggling (2) †	1 hour, 1 minute
Joggling/fast marathon (1)	26.2 miles / 3 hours, 22 minutes
Joggling/distance (1)	50 miles / 1 hour
Squats (6)	4,495 / 1 hour
Burpees (squat thrusts) (2)	1,649 / 1 hour
Hopscotch (2)	390 games / 24 hours
Yodeling (1)	27 hours
Brick carrying (2)	71 miles
Basketball dribbling (2)	96.5 miles/24 hours
Backwards unicycling (1)	53.71 miles
Step-ups (2)	2,574/1 hour
Glass balancing (1)	57 glasses on chin
Largest bouquet (1)	27,713 flowers

† There is no longer a Guinness record for this.

Because It's There

Sometimes you're inspired to do something great. Why? Because it fills you with awe. Because you love it. Because it's there.

Youngest to Climb all 50 Peaks

At 14, Joshua Stewart was the youngest person to climb to the highest point in each of the 50 states.

How he did it

Granite Peak, in Montana, was Joshua's first state peak. From there Joshua's climbing took him and his father (who is the 50th person to climb all the peaks) zig-zagging around the United States. Not all the "peaks" were tough climbs: "Florida's – 435 feet – is just a hill off the side of a road." But Mount McKinley, in Alaska, was a different story. "We were on it for three weeks," Joshua recalls. "Sometimes we had to stay in our tent for five days at a time, because of the snowstorms. We had to go out and shovel the snow off our tent or we'd suffocate." When Joshua reached the top, he would be the youngest to climb Mount McKinley – or so he thought. On the way up, he met a girl three weeks younger, who was just coming down.

Dream Record

"I'm working on climbing the highest mountains in each continent. I've already done Kilimanjaro in Africa and Mt. McKinley in North America."

TRY THIS!

Rick Hansen wheeled 24,901.55 miles through four continents and 34 countries. How far can you go in your wheelchair?

Cheri Becerra was one of a record 3,300 athletes with disabilities who competed at the 1996 Paralympics Games in Atlanta, Georgia. 225 new world records were set.

⬡ Highest High-Wire Walk

Philippe Petit walked a wire stretched 1,350 feet above the ground between the World Trade Towers, on August 7, 1974.

How he did it

This is how Petit himself tells it:

"Amazingly enough, this artist (who learned by himself the art of wire walking) had a dream to put a wire across some of the most magnificent buildings in the world. And so he decided to try the World Trade Towers. He didn't tell anyone, because he knew he wouldn't get permission. Instead, he studied the buildings for nine years to decide where and how to set up his wire.

"His goal was not to be rich and famous, but to give a theatrical performance for the 100,000 people who stopped that morning to watch. The appeal of flying and climbing is in the heart of men forever and strikes early. A wire walker is like a bird. The question still remains: Why did he do it? I've never answered the question. Instead I turn it into a question. Do you ask an artist why he paints? I am not a stuntman or a daredevil. I am a highwire artist."

Extra Young

In 1997, Tara Lipinski, age 14, became the youngest figure skater to win the World Championship. "I was just happy that it happened," she says, "It didn't matter about age."

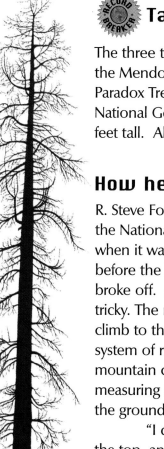

⬡ Tallest Tree

The three tallest trees in the world are the Mendocino tree, 367.5 feet tall; the Paradox Tree, 366.3 feet tall; and the National Geographic Society Tree, 365.5 feet tall. All are in northern California.

How he does it

R. Steve Foster drew this picture of the National Geographic Society tree when it was the world's tallest tree, before the leader (the tallest sprig) broke off. Measuring very tall trees is tricky. The most accurate way is to climb to the top of the tree – using a system of ropes like those used by mountain climbers – and drop a measuring tape or tool down to the ground.

"I dropped down ten feet from the top, and drew the top of the tree. Then I dropped down another ten feet and drew the next section." On and on, until he reached the forest floor. "I went back up several times to check and redraw," says Steve. "All in all it took two weeks." It was no trouble for Steve, who loves trees so much he lives in one: his home is a three-level tree house in the Oregon woods.

Because It's Out There

You don't have to be a rocket scientist to guess that space flight is a big record breaker.

Longest Time in Space

Astronaut Shannon W. Lucid spent 188 days in space – more than any woman.

How she did it

Lucid's record-breaking mission began when space shuttle Atlantis took off from Kennedy Space Center on March 22, 1996. The shuttle docked with Russia's Mir Space Station, and Lucid climbed aboard. She spent the next six months on Mir, until astronaut John W. Blaha arrived to replace her, and Atlantis took her home.

Lucid also holds the record for most space flights for a woman: five. After her first flight she said, "It was the longest time of my entire life without a book to read. Now that's a record." By the time Lucid reached Mir, she had solved that problem: "My book nook!" A strap on the wall of a passageway held her book, and she wedged herself against the wall to read. So, what did she miss this time? "Potato chips!"

Most Flights in Space

As of June, 1997, two space shuttle Earth orbiters are tied for having the most flights: Columbia and Discovery have logged 22 flights each.

How they do it

It was Columbia that became the first orbiter to rocket into space and return by touching down on a runway as gently as any airplane. That was in 1981. Since then, the space shuttle fleet has flown over 243 million miles – more than the distance to the sun – and back. These powerful flying machines are far lighter than a train locomotive – but have much more horsepower, the thrust it takes to escape Earth's atmosphere and to orbit it.

Dream Record

If all goes well, the 90th shuttle flight will lift off in April, 1998. It will be the 25th journey for Columbia. More shuttle flights are already in the works – and plans are set up to the turn of the century.

EXTRA Tall

The doors of the vehicle Assembly Building at Kennedy Space Center are 460 feet high. The building was used to build the tall Saturn rockets used in the Apollo, Skylab, and Apollo/Soyuz space programs. These days the building is used to stack space shuttle parts.

TRY THIS!

The youngest astronaut was Sally Ride, who took off in space shuttle Challenger at age 32 years, 23 days.

Could you pogo on the moon? Turn the page.

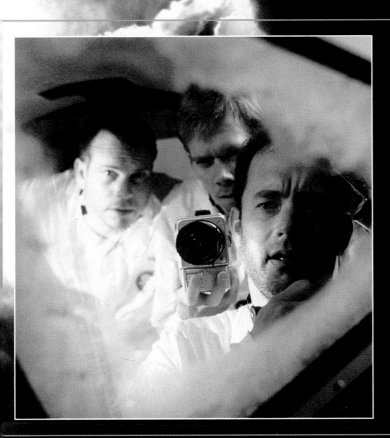

Farthest Person from Earth

No one has ever been as far from Earth as the Apollo 13 astronauts – Captain James Lovell, Jr., Fred Haise, Jr., and John L. Swigert – were on April 14, 1970. Their fateful flight took them 248, 655 miles from Earth.

How they did it

Apollo 13's mission was to land on the moon, not go around it, but that's exactly what they had to do. The reason? An explosion in an oxygen tank set their spaceship spinning and lurching off course on its way to the moon. Suddenly the mission became a struggle to survive. Because of the way the ship was powered, turning straight around would have taken too much energy. Instead, the astronauts charted a course that took them in a giant loop behind the moon. At left, a scene from *Apollo 13*, the movie based on the real-life drama.

What Goes Up...

...must come down, someday!
To keep a ball in the air, you have
to defy gravity.

Most Kicks, Doubles

Tricia George and Gary Lautt
kicked their footbag 123,456
times in a row. It took them
nearly 20 hours.

How they did it

To keep a footbag in the air, you have to get your
feet off the ground and keep the footbag in the air.
It's tough to do it for five minutes – but all day?
Working with a partner adds risk. And how do you
practice when you live hundreds of miles apart?

To get ready for their record attempt, Tricia
and Gary practiced kicking the footbag separately.
Then Tricia traveled from her home in Clackamas,
Oregon, to practice with Gary in Chico, California.
"We worked out for two hours at a time, doing
15,000 kicks." They planned their record attempt,
scheduling breaks for rest, food, and the bathroom.
"We did 20 kicks each, then passed the footbag,"
says Tricia.

How many kicks would they be able
to do? That number was still up in the air.
Once they reached 100,000 kicks, it was
hard to stop. "We shot for 111,111.
Then we decided we liked the
look of 123,456 even better!"

Juggling Rings

Albert Lucas, who's been juggling since
he could stand up, is one of two people
in the world who can keep 12 rings in
the air at a time. His next attempt
– 14 rings – will take place at the
Massachusetts Institute
of Technology (MIT),
where scientists think
it can't be done.

How he does it

"The first rings you throw up have
to be the fastest," Lucas says.
"It's like getting a rocket off the
launching pad: the first 300 feet are
the hardest, but after that a little
extra thrust moves you forward."

Scientists have studied the
problem of juggling rings. "They think
there's a top number that can be kept
in the air at once, based on the pull of
Earth's gravity – and they don't think
more than 12 is possible." But more
than 12 is Lucas's dream – and he
might have to leave Earth to do it!

Dream Record

"Earth's gravity is eight times as strong as
the moon's. On the moon, rings would
come down much slower. And there's
no air there to move the rings. If I made
a perfect, straight throw, the ring might
go 30 feet – compared to 10 on Earth.
On the moon, there's no telling how
many rings I could keep in the
air at once!"

The Vanguard 1 Satellite (below) was launched March 17, 1958. It was the second "successful" U.S. satellite. Successful means "it stayed up" – and boy, did it! Just 16.5 cm in diameter (6 feet, 5 inches), Vanguard 1 is still in orbit (circling) around the Earth. The rocket that launched Vanguard is still up there, too – and it's the oldest piece of space equipment in orbit.

How they do it

The 8,000 satellites orbiting Earth were lifted into space by rockets or space shuttles. They used their own rockets to move into a higher path of orbit around the Earth. Next came the tricky part: staying there.

Flying objects have to beat gravity's pull to stay up. On Earth, footbags, balls, and rings get their power from people. In space, satellites – like the Salyut VII space station shown above right – are powered by rocket engines. If push from the engine matches the pull of gravity, then the satellite's path matches the curve of the Earth. The satellite stays in orbit, instead of shooting into space or falling to Earth.

TRY THIS!

The "keepy-uppy" distance — for keeping a soccer ball up while running — was set by Jan Skorkovsky of the Czech Republic: 26 miles 385 yards. Here, Rob Walters — a former record-holder who's trying to catch up — practices for his next try.

Pop! Splat!

Bubble, bubble, toil and trouble. It's made of something thin and light, but strong enough to hold air. And if you can get it to do what you want, you might just set a record.

 ## Biggest Bubble Gum Bubble

Susan Montgomery Williams blew a bubble 23 inches in diameter

How she does it

"I chew plain pink original flavor gum," Susan says. "Just three pieces — it doesn't take a gigantic wad of gum to blow a big bubble. I chew it until the sugar is gone, and when it's rubbery and hard, I blow. I blow very slowly, while moving the gum to the front of my mouth." She pinches her bubble on each end to keep it off her hair and face, and continues blowing gently. "That way, if a wind comes up, I have control of the bubble."

Susan broke her first bubble record at age 17, at the Bubble Yum contest (see Try This) and has kept on blowing away the competition ever since. When will her record be broken? "I'm looking for some real gumpetition," says Susan.

Splat! There goes another record!

14

Longest Balloon Flight

Steve Fossett flew 9,672 miles in 146 hours and 54 minutes – just over six days.

How he did it

Steve Fossett took off from Busch Stadium in St. Louis, Missouri on January 13, 1997. His balloon, called "Solo Spirit" landed six days later in Piparpur, India. He was trying to fly around the world without landing, something no balloonist has ever done. The planned route, following the jet stream, would take him across northern Africa and southern Europe – or so he thought. While flying, Fossett got word that the government of Libya would not let him fly through its airspace. Fossett had to change his route, using valuable fuel that he needed to cross the Pacific Ocean. He kept going as long as he could, enduring thunderstorms, lack of sleep, and fierce cold.

This flight was Steve Fossett's second attempt to fly around the world in a hot-air balloon. During the winter of 1996-1997 two other balloonists tried – and failed – to circle the globe. None got as far as Fossett.

TRY THIS!

A contestant at the Bubble Yum bubble-blowing competition shows how a bubble is measured. Calipers (the big cardboard scissor) measure it from the center of one side to the other. The measurement includes the bubble's curve.

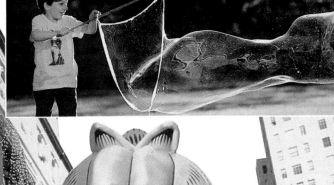

EXTRA Long

The longest soap bubble ever blown was 105 feet long. Alan McKay, of Wellington, New Zealand, made it using a bubble wand, dishwashing soap, glycerine, and water.

Biggest Parade Balloon

Garfield the cat is the largest latex balloon to appear in Macy's Thanksgiving Day parade in New York City. At 61 feet long and 35 feet wide, Garfield holds 18,907 cubic feet of helium and air.

How they do it

Garfield has been flying along the streets of New York since 1984. His "skin" is made of nearly 450 pounds of nylon, which is coated on both sides with urethane and heat sealed so air won't leak out. Macy's parade balloons are made in Hoboken, New Jersey, at a giant factory that used to make Tootsie Rolls.

How much helium and how much air goes into the balloons depends on the weather. The afternoon and night before Thanksgiving, all the balloons are blown up and tested. Their chief designer, Manfred G. Bass, is on hand to help balloon captains get their "giant toys" up and flying. It's thanks to the "little people" – the balloon handlers who man ropes holding Garfield – that the big cat stays out of trouble as he passes between the buildings, around lightposts, and under wires.

Buzzzzzzooooom!

How do these record breakers do what they do? They've got the rest of us — including some scientists — scratching our heads!

 Most Parachute Jumps

Don Kellner has made 22,750 jumps — and counting!

How he does it

Don Kellner can tell you the facts of how he keeps the parachuting record: his wife Darlene keeps flying their plane, and he keeps on jumping out of it. What's harder to tell is how parachuting feels. "You can't practice for it, and you can't do anything in the world to equal it. You jump out of the airplane and there you are, in the sky. You don't think of work, problems, anything." The big, square 'chutes Kellner uses let him travel several miles before landing gently on the ground. The parachute fights the pressure of air caused as the person is pulled down by gravity, and this slows the fall.

Does it get boring after, say, 10,000 jumps? No way! "I'm scared to death each time I leave the airplane, but I have to keep doing it. There are no words to describe the feeling." Even so, now and then Kellner tries something a little different. This picture shows his 15,000th jump – from the basket of a hot-air balloon.

 **Fastest Jet**

Jet speeds are usually compared to the speed of sound, called Mach. A Lockheed SR-71 flew at Mach 3 (three times the speed of sound) for 2,982 miles.

How it does it

The SR-71 is built of titanium, a metal with the strength of steel, but the light weight of aluminum. "When you see it on the ground before takeoff, when the titanium is still cold, you see fuel leaking from the belly of the aircraft," says Lieutenant Wilson Camelo, of Beale Air Force Base. As the jet reaches high speed, it gets hotter – and the titanium expands. "The leading edges reach 700 to 800 degrees Fahrenheit. During flight, the jet grows six inches because of the heat. It welds itself together in the air."

Fastest and Slowest Wing Beats

1. A South American hummingbird called the horned sungem beats its wings 90 times per second – faster than any other bird.

2. The swallowtail butterfly beats its wings 300 beats per minute, slower than any other insect.

How they do it

For years, scientists watched moths, bumblebees, and butterflies fly, and thought, "Impossible!" But now they've discovered that the pattern an insect's wings beat into the air gives it the extra lift it needs to stay up. As the wings flap down, air flows over them in a spiral that grows with every flap. The air spiral sucks the wings up again so the insect doesn't sink.

It's easier to see why hummingbirds are champion fliers that can fly backward, forward, and upside down. These birds have extra-light bones and extra-strong chest muscles – their flying muscles. Other birds get power only when their wings beat down. But hummingbirds are the only birds that have muscles for raising *and* lowering their wings – so they get power from both beats.

EXTRA Wingspan

Students in Hampton, Virginia, built the largest paper airplane in America, with a wingspan of 30 feet, 6 inches. It flew 114 feet, 9 inches.

TRY THIS!

The record for skipping stones across water is 38 skips.

Come Out and Play!

It started out as a game. It ended up in *The Guinness Book of World Records*. To all you players out there: Play on!

Make a game of setting a record — like Ashrita.

 ## Most People Playing Twister

In 1987, 4,160 students at the University of Massachusetts at Amherst played Twister. The winner? Allison Culler held out through the whole game.

How they do it

Start with a math problem: for every four people playing your game, you need a Twister mat. So if 5,000 students tried to break the record, they'd need 1,500 Twister mats. And each of those mats takes up 5 feet 6 inches x 4 feet 6 inches of space. Hmmm, let's see now...

You get the idea: setting up a Twister record attempt takes time and planning. Mark Morris, of Milton Bradley (the company that makes Twister) says, "You need space, and a lot of people. But you only need one spinner!" Want to try? See page 64.

Youngest Chess Master

Vijay Bhat, of San Jose, California, was 10 when he became a chess master – which means he earned a rating of 2,200 points by playing tournament games against tough players.

How he does it

"I've been playing in tournaments since I was 6 1/2," says Vijay, now 12. "My mother taught me when I was four. She had learned from *her* parents." Playing with his mother helped, because most of the high-rated players Vijay plays are adults. "They don't give me a hard time, because they know it doesn't come easy. You have to work hard at it."

Although Vijay doesn't play chess every day, he studies chess every day, reading through and imagining the moves made in grand master games. "If you lose your focus during a game, you could make bad moves and lose. You have to be able to concentrate, and be patient."

TRY THIS!

The highest skateboard jump was 11 feet 8 inches by Sergei Ventura of the United States. Try it off a ramp as Sergei did, but don't forget your helmet and pads!

C₃ R₁ A₁ Z₁₀ I₁ E₁ S₁ T₁

Highest Scrabble Score

Phil Appleby scored 1,094 points in one game. The most ever scored in the U.S. for one word was 311 points. One of the words that scored 311 was CRAZIEST. The player used two triple word squares and used all seven of his letters.

How they do it

Joe Edley, two-time national Scrabble champion and 1997 number-one rated player, says, "You can't be a top player without studying words." Edley uses a computer program that scrambles words for him to figure out. But first, he studies the dictionary and finds words. "You might not know what ulus are," he says, "but if you go to Alaska, they sell them in stores!" (An ulu is a knife.)

You have to keep your feelings under control, too, Edley says. "No matter how good you are, you can't play without losing. In the darkest hour of a tournament, after you've lost three games, you can still come back and win!"

EXTRA Spin

The world's largest yo-yo measured 10 feet 4 inches in diameter and weighed 897 pounds. It was hoisted by a 187-foot crane which bounced to yo-yo it four times.

Amusement Parks

Whether you're looking for big thrills or a gentle ride, amusement parks are the place to go for a record-breaking good time.

 ## Largest Amusement Park

Walt Disney World, located in Orange and Osceola Counties, Florida (southwest of Orlando), covers 30,000 acres.

How it does it

Walt Disney World owns and has plans for all the land, although 12,000 acres are not yet built on. The giant park includes the Magic Kingdom, Epcot, Disney-MGM Studios, Walt Disney World International Sports Complex, Disney's Animal Kingdom (opening in 1998), golf courses, hotels, and more.

Dream Record

A design team in London dreams of building a 500 foot ferris wheel to celebrate the year 2000. Will they do it? Watch and see!

EXTRA Sky-High

The largest ferris wheel in the U.S. is the Texas Star at Fair Park in Dallas, Texas. It stands 212 feet 6 inches high.

Fastest and Tallest Roller Coaster

Superman, at Six Flags Magic Mountain in Valencia, California, has a tower 415 feet tall. Its cars go 100 mph at top speed.

How it does it

Superman is so fast because it's so tall. "The ride is L-shaped," says Six Flags vice president Jim Blackie. The tower is made from an extra light steel called HSLA – **h**igh **s**trength **l**ow **a**lloy steel – which reinforces the tower against wind and earthquakes. The tower was built in 40-foot sections, then lifted into place by a huge crane.

A roller coaster car pulls up to the top of this tower slowly – right under Superman's nose – and drops FAST. "It's zero gravity coming down, kind of an astronaut feeling," says Blackie. This means that if you hold something in front of you as you drop, it'll stay right where it is. It won't fly up or down. "Most people look straight forward. If you look to either side, it's quite terrifying." Blackie has ridden Superman more than 50 times. In the curve at the corner of the L, the gravity force is 4 G's – or four times usual. "It's the combination of safety and terror that people love," Blackie says. "When they get off, they're pumped up and jazzed and screaming."

Oldest Carousel in the U.S.

The horses on the carousel at the end of Main Street in Watch Hill, Rhode Island, are the oldest in the United States. They date back to the 1860s.

How they do it

To establish this record, Gary Anderson had to solve a mystery: where did the carousel horses come from, and who built them? It started when Anderson, an artist, was asked to restore the horses. He went looking for some like it to match his painting with – and found rocking horses that had been patented in 1861 by Andrew Christian. "These horses had red leather manes, tails, and saddles, like Christian's. Later carousel horses had less leather, real horsehair, and carved saddles." When the rocking horses didn't sell, Anderson says, Christian got together with Charles Dare, who built carousels – and the result was the little dirt-floor carousel in Watch Hill.

In the 1800's, the carousel was turned by a horse pulling a rope. Everybody in Watch Hill remembers riding on it as a kid, but nobody knows how it got there. "A story has been passed down that a traveling circus left the little carousel behind," says Anderson.

Building Bonanza

A grain of sand, a playing card, a brick, a giant stone. What can you do with these? If you're a builder, you know: set records!

Tallest Sand Castle

The tallest sand castle stood 21 feet, 6 inches high.

How they do it

Take a good look at the pictures on this page. You're seeing all the tools that sand castle builders use: buckets, shovels, a few pieces of wood, water, and their own two hands. At top right, hoses help workers soak a giant mound of sand. Sand sculptors need to keep their sand just wet enough to mold, just dry enough to stay up. If it gets too wet... sand slide! At bottom right, a sculptor carefully cuts away extra sand from a turret. And that guy on the left? That's Ashrita Furman, demonstrating his brick carrying record. Fits right in, doesn't he?

Longest Wall

The main line of the Great Wall of China stretches 2,150 miles across northern China. Its branches make up an extra 2,195 miles. It extends from Gansu province to the Yellow Sea in the east.

How they did it

The Great Wall was built by many, many people, each carrying bricks or pulling carts full of stones and dirt. Work began around 221 B.C. during the reign of Shi Huangdi of the Qin dynasty, who wanted to protect southern China from invaders from the north. Shi began by uniting smaller walls that had already been built in several Chinese states. The result: the Great Wall is so big that it can be seen from the moon.

Largest Lego Model in U.S.

Clock Boy is 22 feet high. He keeps time, playing "Yankee Doodle" on the hour.

How she does it

Francie Berger is the model design supervisor at Lego, "When people asked me what I wanted to do when I grew up, I said I would be an architect," says Francie. "I didn't think I could do a job building Lego." But she did! As an architecture student, she sent a proposal to Lego, which used to get all its models from the home country, Denmark. "I thought that models for the U.S. should be made here." Now they are – by Francie! "The biggest problem is to make round shapes from square bricks. We draw the outline of a model and use graph paper to figure out how to make the curves." Big models need to be supported on the inside by foundations of bricks. Lego designers rarely use the specialty pieces that come in certain kits. "Our rule is that any movement a model does has to be something a child could do by hand or with a Lego motor." That's true of Clock Boy, who stands in the Mall of America (the biggest in the U.S.)

TRY THIS!

Bryan Berg's record house of cards stood 19 feet 2 inches high and was 100 stories tall. Bryan learned to build card houses when he was little. "My brother used to stomp through the room, so I learned to build strong towers," says Bryan.

23

Making It Work

Machines **are a way that people make** the forces of the world **work for us. Some machines** do things people can't do for themselves. And others? Well...

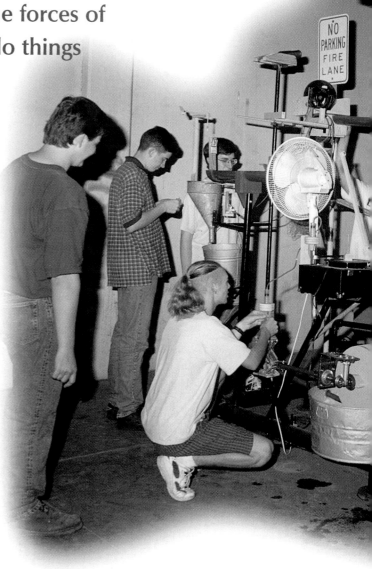

Dream Record

A team of students at Monache High School in Porterville, California, are working on the world's largest Rube Goldberg machine. When done, it will have 100 steps in a chain reaction that leads to one marvelous act: turning out the lights.

How they're doing it

"You drop a coin in the slot, and it makes the toilet flush, and the water runs into a pan that turns a water wheel..." That's how Adam Mitchell, 17, describes the start of the chain reaction he and nine friends have been working on for months. "My favorite part is a marble that shoots into a funnel and eventually connects two wires." Sounds simple, but... "I had to design a spring-loaded trigger that would shoot the marble 10 to 15 feet. I decided to use a ball bearing instead of a marble."

Teacher Kinsey Blomgren says, "When you have a series of steps that are all connected, you want to have it all working – every step." If just one step doesn't work, the whole machine won't work. When done, the machine will be built on six sections of frames made of steel pipes. It will stand eight feet high and 50 feet long. That's a long way to go to turn off the lights!

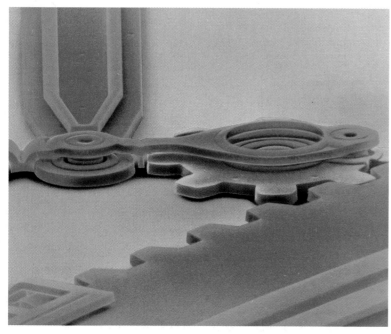

 ## World's Smallest Machine

A tiny gear that's part of a microscopic machine is only 50 microns across — the same diameter as a hair — and was made by Sandia National Laboratories in New Mexico.

How they do it

"It's called a microengine," says engineer Ernest Garcia. The tiny motor was first made to be used as part of a weapon. It was made through a process called photo-lithography, the same process that's used to make tiny transistors and circuits. Photolithography uses light to cut tiny shapes out of silicon wafers.

"Because it's so small, we can drive it faster than any other electrically driven device – about 300,000 RPM (revolutions per minute)." The little engine can drive extremely small machines – something that could never be done before. "You could drive machinery to inspect the insides of things you can't usually get to, like the human body."

Largest Solar Electric Power Plant

The Harper Lake Site in the Mojave Desert of California covers 1,280 acres and produces 160 megawatts (MW) of electricity.

How it does it

The plant is powered by 6,500 mirrors stretched across a huge field. Computers track the sun's position and change the way the mirrors are angled in relation to it.

The sun's energy is used to heat a fluid in tubes traveling to the giant steam turbine (below). When the fluid reaches 735 degrees F, it drives the steam generators to create electricity.

Extra Beetles

More Volkswagen Beetles have been produced than any other car: 21 million, as of 1996. Beetles are built now only in Puebla, Mexico. A new Beetle is planned in the U.S. before the year 2000.

Extra Hot

The Princeton Tokamak Fusion Test Reactor in Princeton, New Jersey, is one hot machine. It was used to mix deuterium and tritirium plasma, which fused at 918 million degrees F — ten times hotter than the sun. Here, scientists check the machine before running it.

I Get Around

You can go around a track or around the world. Just go for that record!

EXTRA Miniature

The smallest model car in the world is a tiny Toyota. Its bumper is 50 microns thick. The car, with a motor 1 mm across, can drive at 1/100th of a mile per hour.

EXTRA Small

Jeff Gibson's car, the "Arbet", is the smallest street-legal car in the United States. The car, built by Arliss Sluder, is just 88 3/4 inches long and 40 1/2 inches wide.

 Youngest Women's Motocross Champion

Kristy Shealy, age 14, won the women's division in the 1993 AMA Amateur/Youth National Motocross.

How she did it

Kristy started riding at three, when she had a Suzuki motorcycle with training wheels. She entered her first motocross at six. There weren't many girls or women in the sport, and there still aren't. At first it freaked me out, all those little boys riding so fast," she said. "But it made me competitive, too. I work to get faster every day." At top speed, motocross racers go between 50 and 65 miles per hour.

"I work on my riding skills with a trainer, who teaches me a lot of attitude, too. My mind has to be in top shape to race. I have to say to myself, 'These guys are not better than me.' I can run with them!"

Walk Around the World

Dave Kunst left his home in Wasica, Minnesota, on June 20, 1970, and returned home on July 27, 1974. He was the first person to walk around the world: 14,452 miles in all.

How he did it

Dave and his brother John set out for the Atlantic Ocean with a mule named Willie-make-it and a dream. "John and I had watched people walk on the moon in 1969 – just one year before – and we wanted to do something nobody's ever done before."

They touched the Atlantic in New York, then took a plane to Portugal and touched the ocean on the other side. Equipped with a second mule (Willie-make-it II), they began the long trek across Europe and Asia. In Afghanistan, disaster struck. Bandits who thought they had money with them attacked them. Both brothers were shot, and John died. While Dave was recovering, another brother, Pete, arrived from the U.S. and came along on the walk to the Indian Ocean.

Dave and Pete crossed the ocean to Australia before Pete returned home. In the Australian desert, Will Willie-make-it, the third mule, died. That's when Dave met an Australian schoolteacher who was driving across the country. She slowed down to let her car (nicknamed Will-she-make-it) carry Dave's things, and drove beside Dave. Along the way, the two fell in love. But Dave's

journey wasn't done. He touched the Pacific Ocean, then crossed it to California. He and Will Willie-make-it II (the fourth mule!) continued home to Wasica.

"I walked 20 million steps," Dave says, figuring 31 steps per 100 feet. "I wore out 21 pairs of shoes. But I proved something to myself: If a human being makes up his mind, is determined, sets goals, he can walk around the world."

EXTRA Swift

In 1997 Jeff Gordon won the Daytona 500 at just 25 years, 6 months of age. He was the youngest ever to do so.

TRY THIS!

Bud Badyna ran a 10km race backward in 45 minutes, 37 seconds.

You could also try riding a unicycle backward. Ashrita did!

Learning Through Language

Talk. **Listen.** Sing. **Whisper. Sign.**
Write. Learn. **Set Records.**

Oldest Classroom Map

Johnston Elementary School in Appleton, Wisconsin has the oldest classroom map in the United States. The map, dated 1885, was printed between 1886 and 1893. It has hung on the walls of Appleton classrooms for over 100 years.

How they did it

"We knew our map was kind of old," says Leigh Sinclair, 11. "There's no Panama Canal marked on it. It spells Korea *Corea*. It says *Sandwich Islands* instead of Hawaii. And the capital of Norway was *Christiana*, instead of Oslo." When the map was first hung in an Appleton classroom, Appleton was a small logging town. Main Street was four blocks long, and the school was a one-room school house. Now the town has 16 elementary schools, but Johnston – named for Appleton's first settler – has the old map.

"We weren't sure it was the oldest around," says teacher James Klimaszewski. The school entered their map in a contest held by Rand McNally, the map maker. Their map won! The map, its colors faded and its fabric torn, speaks for the way people of the times saw the world. "There was no Antarctica," says Leigh. "Not even the South Pole."

EXTRA Studious

Michael Kearney, of Los Angeles, California, is the youngest person to graduate from college. He was 6 years, 7 months, when he started college, and 10 years, 4 months when he graduated from the University of South Alabama.

Most People Signing

It was some finale: 250 children signed and sang "Somewhere Over the Rainbow" at the Swan Theater in High Wycombe, England.

How they did it

"Every year the Swan has a Summer Youth Project," says the theater's Joy Campbell. "There's another group in the area called the Young Deaf Activities Group." In 1996, the two groups decided to get together. The deaf group taught the Swan singers to sign the last song in their performance of *The Wizard of Oz*. "They came and taught us during two lunchtime sessions," Campbell says. "It was a mixture of British Sign Language and a visual presentation— because not all the words and ideas have signs." The groups didn't plan to set a record. "We wanted to help children see that deaf people have another language and way of life of their own. When someone said we might have set a record, I said, 'Ha, ha!' But they were right!"

EXTRA Long

A bottle with a message inside was dropped near the island of Foula, Scotland, on June 12, 1914. It was found 82 years later, on August 21, 1996, in a fisherman's nets, just 5 miles away.

Colonel Ernest Loftus began his diary on May 14, 1896, at age 12 and continued it until the day he died – July 7, 1987 (age 103!) No diary has ever been kept longer.

EXTRA Old

The letter O has not changed in shape since 1300 B.C. when it became part of the Phoenician alphabet.

...OR THIS!

The longest story ever written with every word beginning with the same letter was *Olgin Ostrov (Olga's Island)* written by Nikolai Kultyatov. It had 16,000 words, all beginning with the letter O.

Making Money

What's the value of holding a record? These record-breakers are worth their weight in gold.

⬡ Most Expensive Teddy

Teddy Girl, a Steiff bear made in 1904, was sold for £110,000 ($171,578).

How they do it

When a lot of people want to buy the same thing, the price goes up. When that thing is rare, the demand for it becomes even higher. A lot of people wanted Teddy Girl, a bear made by the Steiff Company. She belonged to Bob Henderson when he was a little boy, and stayed in good condition even though both Bob and his younger brother Charles played with her. By the time Teddy Girl was sold, in 1994, there were very few bears like her left.

Teddy Girl was one of the first bears Steiff made with joints that moved, and she had a story. People who collect antiques like to know where the antiques have been, who they've belonged to and what they meant to their owners. Teddy Girl's history was a big attraction to those who came to her auction. Even the owners of the auction house, Christie's of London, were astonished as the bids for Teddy Girl went higher and higher. She was bought by a Japanese man, Yoshihiro Sekiguchi.

 ## Longest Piggy Bank

Penny the Pig stands 6 feet 11 inches high and is 17 feet 2 inches long.

How they did it

Penny was built by Mary Ann Spanagel, an artist in Indiana, Pennsylvania. Spanagel is an artist for a local amusement park. She specializes in making floats for parades and other giant objects. Penny was made of 25 yards of fibreglass. It took 320 hours to build her.

Coldwell Banker Real Estate asked Spanagel to make a giant piggy bank they could use to gather donations. At first, the money Penny collected was given to Habitat for Humanity, an organization that builds houses for homeless people. Now, Penny is loaned out to all kinds of charities.

Penny is so high that it would be dangerous to ask people to put money in a slot on her back. Instead, givers climb a ladder to Penny's snout and feed cash into her nostrils. The money slides down a funnel into her stomach, which can be unlocked and opened later.

 ## Most Valuable Pile of Coins

The YWCA of Seattle, King County, Washington, collected 1,000,298 coins worth $126,463.61.

How they did it

It took five months and many, many, donations. "You'd think if everyone just brought their spare change in jars, you'd have millions," says Kerry Coughlin of the YWCA. "But it really doesn't add up that fast." The YWCA asked for donations to be given in coin form. Every penny counted. "The kindergartner who opened his little paw and gave three cents meant a lot to us."

The best part of breaking this record? Spending the money! The YWCA used it to help build Family Village, which has houses, job services, and a daycare centre for homeless families. That plan helped the money add up quickly. "People even had birthday parties and asked for contributions, instead of presents," Coughlin says. Family Village supports families as they move from needing help to taking care of themselves. "We've helped hundreds of people," Coughlin says.

EXTRA Shopping

The biggest mall in the world is the West Edmonton Mall in Alberta, Canada. The building is 5.2 million square feet, built on 121 acres of land. It houses 800 stores and services, including 11 major department stores. The parking lots have space for 20,000 cars. 20 million shoppers pass through each year.

Dean Gould of Felixstowe, England can snatch 328 coins off his elbow. He owes his coin-snatching record to the way he stacks the coins – overlapping them into a short, thick stack just the size to fit into his hand. Start with a small stack – and work up!

From Top to Toe

No, there's no record for smelliest socks or holiest sneakers. But clothes can make records in other ways. Read clothesly!

Most Expensive Costume Sho

Dorothy's ruby slippers from the 1939 movie *The Wizard of Oz* sold to a mystery buyer at Christie's in New York City. The price tag? $165,000!

Largest Hat on Stage

This hat from the San Francisco stage show *Beach Blanket Babylon* stands 33 feet high and 20 feet long. It weighs 285 pounds.

How they do it

Actress Val Diamond wore the hat – called "The City of San Francisco" – in the 20th anniversary production of Steve Silver's *Beach Blanket Babylon*. "You don't feel like you're wearing it," she says. It's more like the hat is wearing her. "You're just a part of it, it's so big. You can't really move it by yourself, so you're kind of helped along." Are there cables? Wires? Weights? Only the *Beach Blanket Babylon* backstage artists know for sure – and they won't tell.

"The hats are made mostly out of pressboard and feathers," says the show's general manager, Link King. King won't say any more than that about how the hats stay on the actors' heads. More than 80 colossal hats have appeared in the bright, colorful show since it first hit the stage. Actors have worn lamp posts, pizza boxes, ice cream sundaes, the U.S. Capitol Building, Christmas trees, and wedding cakes. Val Diamond, the show's star, is working on her own record. She's been with *Beach Blanket Babylon* for more than 20 years. "I'll keep going as long as I can wear the hats!" she says.

How they do it

You'd think the high price of Dorothy's slippers might have something to do with the cost of the rubies. But they weren't real rubies. And they weren't magic – outside of Oz.

The trick of the collector's trade is demand. The fact that lots of people wanted the slippers made them valuable. When Christie's sold them at auction, they started the bidding at a number they were sure they'd get. Then, people who wanted the shoes raised their bids. The highest bidder bought the shoes.

Extra Big
Matthew McGrory wears size 26 shoes.

World's Biggest Bib Overalls

These big bibs were 14 feet long – almost two stories high – and had a 96-inch waist.

How they did it

Back in 1917, the William Webber dry goods store in Murphyville, Illinois, was a big seller of bib overalls. Webber wanted to advertise his business by making a pair of bibs that would tower over them all. He special-ordered them from OshKosh B'Gosh, a clothing manufacturer that has been in business since 1895. Oshkosh made Webber's bibs the same way it made others – from blue denim.

To fit Webber's overalls, a person would have had to be 15 feet 6 inches tall. Since Webber couldn't find anyone to fit the bibs, he made a giant clothesline. This photo shows the bibs "marching" in the 4th of July parade.

TRY THIS!

Mata Jagdamba, of Ujjain, India, has hair 13 feet 10 1/2 inches long.

33

Foodarama

What could be greater than food? More food! Enough to give you a stomach ache (or a record).

You've got to *count it...*

...keep coming

Largest Box of Popcorn

The largest box of popcorn ever popped was 7,466 cubic feet, done by kids at Pittsville Elementary School, in Pittsville, Wisconsin.

How to do it

Kids from Beauclerc Elementary School – an earlier record holder – show how it's done. Their popcorn and poppers were all donated, and so were the materials to build the box – wood and corrugated cardboard. Children brought poppers from home, and popped corn during class all day.

Early on, someone counted the number of kernels in a gallon of popcorn. After that, the students did multiplication problems to keep track of the number of gallons in their giant box. It took a week to fill the box completely. By the time it was done, the kids were sick of smelling popcorn. A lot of it was stale by then, so it was donated to a pig farm.

WORLD'S LARGEST BOX OF POPCORN

...and *keep track of it* (to make it official)!

Biggest Bagel

This breathtaking bagel weighed 563 pounds. It measured 59 3/16 inches in diameter and was 12 1/2 inches thick. Kraft Foods and Lender's Bagels cooked it in Mattoon, Illinois.

How they did it

"If you're going to build a big bagel, first you have to have a big oven," says Jim Cudahy, plant manager at Lender's Bagels. Getting that oven built was a community effort. Local builders donated the time and materials to build it, and a natural gas company donated the gas to fire it up.

Then Larry Wilkerson – Lender's master baker – started to figure out a recipe. "If you used the normal percentage of yeast," Cudahy says, "the batter would get so big the bagel would explode in the oven." What's more, a normal bagel takes two minutes to boil and 12 minutes to bake. This one took 3 hours to boil and 11 hours to bake. "On the ninth try we finally made it!"

TRY THIS!

Can you grow a giant onion? Compare Mel Ednie's, grown in Fife, Scotland, to the size you usually find in your garden or grocery store. Ednie's weighed 12 pounds, 4 ounces.

Most Tremendous Treat

The biggest Rice Krispie treat weighed 1,413 pounds.

How they did it

Brian Thomas, a baker at the Wood Company, was looking for a good way to celebrate National Rice Month. He thought of Rice Krispie Treats. "Let's make a big one!" he said. "We used 506 pounds of Rice Krispies, 840 pounds of marshmallows, and 117 pounds of margarine."

The cooking started at Lehigh College in Bethlehem, Pennsylvania. "We made it in 40-pound batches," says Thomas. "Folding the Rice Krispies into the melted marshmallow was extremely tiring. We did 10 hours of that!" Chunks of the finished treat were sold to shoppers at a nearby mall. "We made more than $600 to give to local homeless shelters," Thomas says.

Ashrita keeps his eyes on his goal... and his feet on his stilts.

EXTRA Gooey

The largest pizza in the U.S., made by bakers in Havana, Florida, measured 10,057 feet. No, they didn't toss the crust to get it ready for the oven. But there was plenty for everyone.

Down to Earth

Dirt! Garbage! But not just any dirt and garbage. These messes are record-breakers.

 ## World's Largest Landfill

Fresh Kills Landfill, at 2,200 acres, is the world's biggest. It's found on Staten Island, New York City.

How they do it

The Fresh Kills landfill is "filled" like other landfills – with layers of garbage, stones, and soil that go deeper and higher as more trash is laid in. Pipes let gases from deep within the landfill rise to the surface to prevent fires and explosions that might happen if gases built up underground.

Fresh Kills has been in business since 1948, and will have to close soon. Like many other landfills started this century, it's nearly full. Every day, more than 12,000 tons of "new" garbage are added to the landfill. Most of it comes in on barges. Sanitation engineers are working to find new ways of getting rid of trash and to find ways of using already filled land.

 ## Most Recycled Container

Fifty-five percent of all aluminum cans are recycled – more than any other food container.

How they do it

The U.S. Environmental Protection Agency (EPA) keeps track of garbage – and of things that might be thrown in the garbage, but are recycled, instead. "The U.S. is pretty good about recycling," says the EPA's Steve Levy. "Our goal as a planet is to recycle 35% of our waste. Beyond that recycling gets too difficult and costly. The U.S. as a whole does 25%."

Of all the car batteries thrown out, 94% are recycled. Of all the paper used, 58% is recycled. And then there's aluminum. Six out of ten cans are recycled. "People can get money back by recycling cans," Levy explains. And the old cans are easily made into new cans and containers. First, the cans are crushed and pressed into cubes like the one shown below. Then they are shredded into bits, melted down, and remolded into new cans or other aluminum goods.

EXTRA Far-Out

The Mir Space Station is the largest garbage dump in space. Because there's no way to throw things out, trash has built up over 11 years of time in space. Not all the trash is unwanted; because there's no gravity in space, things you put down sometimes just float away. Coming soon: The first space shuttle garbage transport?

EXTRA Stinky

More than 17,000 smells have been identified by scientists. The smelliest substance is ethyl mercaptan, a chemical that smells like rotting cabbage, garlic, onions, burnt toast, and sewer gas...all at once!

Most Cars Washed

Police officers in Walsall, England, washed 2,169 cars in 8 hours – enough to set the British record.

How they did it

Police Constable Ashley Cooper and his team of police did everything right in their record attempt. "The rules said we could have 300 people working, so we made up ten teams of 30. We had ten different washing lines, and had water pumped in for free."

So why is Cooper disappointed? "We wanted to break the world record. We were unsuccessful because not enough cars came. I've sat and thought long and hard about it, and I tell myself, 'We didn't fail.'" The British record is theirs. And another great success? The £10,000 the police raised for charity.

EXTRA Famous

Oscar the Grouch lives in what may be the world's most famous trash can. His television show, Sesame Street, has won more Emmy awards than any other TV show: 64, as of 1996.

Did You See That?

Lights, camera, records! Tune in to these stars of stage and screen. They're Guinness stars, too!

Highest Grossing Film (Re-Issue)

Star Wars, first released in 1977, was re-issued to theaters in 1997. It sold $98.6 million worth of tickets in its first three weeks, more than any other re-issued film.

How they did it

Yes, Jabba the Hutt *is* gross. And yes, he did help *Star Wars* sell. The word *gross* in this record means something else – the total the film sold in tickets.

So how did they do it? Some *Star Wars* fans might say Jabba didn't help at all. After all, he doesn't appear until the second film in the series, *The Empire Strikes Back*, right? Wrong. The film makers knew that people love to hate evil, slimy Jabba, one of the biggest puppets ever made for a film. So they gave him a new scene in the first film. The new scenes brought in people who had seen *Star Wars* plenty of times in theaters – as well as new fans who had never seen *Star Wars* or only knew it on video. The result? A new generation of fans for a favorite movie series.

EXTRA Shine

Shirley Temple (above) won an honorary Oscar at age five. Tatum O'Neal (top) was ten when she won the Best Actress Oscar for *Paper Moon*. And Anna Pacquin (left) won the Best Supporting Actress Oscar at age eleven for her performance in *The Piano*.

Longest Running Broadway Sho

Cats pounced on this record on June 19, 1997, with performance number 6,138. (The show broke the record held by *A Chorus Line*.)   And Marlene Daniel has appeared in over 6,060 shows – more than any other performer in a Broadway musical.

How she does it

Marlene Danielle has 12 pet cats. "They all earn their living," she jokes. "They give me great ideas. I watch them and see their attitudes, and I bring them with me on stage." By the time *Cats* set its record, Danielle had been playing Bombalurina for 15 years.

Danielle admired singer/dancer Tina Turner when she was young, and started her career with several stage roles. "I didn't plan to be a cat for this long!" she admits. With eight performances a week, Danielle makes a point of staying in shape. "Even on a day when I'm not feeling well, I go out there and have a ball. The fact that we're playing animals makes it fun."

Longest Running Animated Series

The Simpsons, with 177 shows – and counting! – passed *The Flintstones* to become the longest running prime time cartoon show on television.

How he does it

"As a kid, I loved it when there were cartoons on in the evening," says Matt Groenig. "I knew kids would love this show because kids love cartoons. I didn't think adults would give the show a chance because cartoons are so silly." But millions of adults are big Simpsons fans. "I think they heard too much laughter from the TV room!" says Groenig.

    The Simpsons, starring Homer and Marge Simpson, and their three children, is nothing like *Leave It to Beaver* or other family shows Groenig watched while growing up. "I said, 'If I get my own TV show it's going to be a lot darker, a lot crazier. I think people understand that even though the Simpsons are not the best examples to live by, they're having a great time. And we're having a great time, telling these stories."

Extra Tunes

The world's largest jukebox, called 'The Wall,' stands in Tokyo, Japan. It's 41 feet 4 inches high and 63 feet wide.

MATT GROENING

The Joys of Toys

Some kids wish for incredible toys. And some grow up to grant their own wishes.

Best-Selling Doll

As of 1997, more than one billion Barbie dolls had been sold worldwide.

How she does it

According to Mattel, the company that makes Barbie, two dolls are sold every second somewhere in the world. If all the world's Barbies were placed head-to-toe, they would circle the world seven times.

The first Barbie was sold in 1959, when the original Teenage Fashion Model came on the market. Ruth Handler had been watching her daughter, Barbara, play with paper dolls. She noticed that Barbie and her friends liked to pretend their dolls were teenagers and adults with exciting lives – including cool clothes, college, and careers. So she started working on a Barbie doll.

More than $1.4 billion worth of Barbies are sold each year. This includes Ken dolls (named for Handler's son Ken). The most popular Barbie ever was Totally Hair Barbie, which came out in 1992. More than ten million dolls sold world-wide.

Biggest Puppet

Mother Earth, made by the Bread and Puppet Theatre, has a head 16 feet high and a body 100 feet long.

How he did it

The artist, Peter Schumann, made Mother Earth's big head by setting seven layers of papier mache over a clay model. Then he reinforced the head with branches, wire, and thin wood called lathe. Mother Earth's body is a big piece of cloth. The head is on a two-wheeled cart with a center pole that acts as the neck. People hold the fabric along the edges to make it billow. There is no structure inside the costume. Instead, the puppeteers make Mother Earth's body seem alive.

"It takes 30 or 40 people to operate Mother Earth," says Elka Schumann, one of the founders of the Bread and Puppet Theatre, which is based in Glover, Vermont. Mother Earth is a favorite in Earth Day parades and other events. "Hundreds can gather under her," says Schumann.

Largest Model Train Set

Northlandz, a model railway, in Flemington, New Jersey, covers 52,000 square feet.

How he did it

"Northlandz was a 25-year project," says Bruce Williams Zaccagnino. For the first twenty-five years, the set was put together piece by piece. Although the trains and tracks were bought, the mountains, valleys, and cities they connect – as well as the bridges and tunnels they run through – are all handmade. Since 1992, Northlandz has been housed in a building built just to hold it. "Pictures can't begin to show all that's here," Zaccagnino says. "There are 3 1/2 levels, and many miles of tracks. It's humungous!"

Northlandz is worth about $9 million in equipment and materials. Zaccagnino, an artist who creates computer games, had to be creative with Northlandz, as well. While he was building it, he had to plan ways to get to all the different sections of it. "Now I can get to any part at any level." How? Hidden passageways – 1 1/2 miles of them! – connect the sections.

EXTRA Steamy

Peggy is the name of the 7 1/4-inch gauge model steam locomotive which covered 167.7 miles in 24 hours at Weston Park, England.

EXTRA Swoosh

Peter DiGiacomo flew a Flexifoil kite at 120 miles per hour in Ocean City, Maryland. The wind, on the front end of Hurricane Andrew, gusted up to 35 mph. The speed of the kite was measured with a radar gun -- the kind police officers use to find out which cars are speeding.

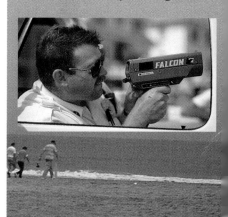

Art Alert

Is there an art to setting records? If you are an artist, there's more than one way to carve out your place in the record book.

Largest Horse Sculpture

This horse-in-the-making stands 24 feet high and weighs 80 tons. Leonardo da Vinci's design of "Il Cavallo" (the horse) is 500 years old.

How they're doing it

In 1482, Leonardo da Vinci was commissioned to build a huge statue by the Duke of Milan, Italy. He designed it and built a clay model, but before he could go on to build the bronze statue, war broke out. The model was destroyed.

In 1977, artist Charles Dent read a magazine article called "The Horse That Never Was." He decided to try to build from Leonardo's designs.

He raised money, had a studio built, and began work. Sadly, Dent died in 1994, before the horse was completed. Now a team of artists and engineers is working to finish the horse. One of them is Skip Kralik. "We've created a plaster shell of the statue, which will be taken apart in sections and cast in bronze. The horse is in full trot," explains Kralik. "So it has to stand on only two legs. It's like raising a sail twenty feet in the air. When the wind blows, all the weight will be pushing at the top, trying to break the horse's legs off." The answer? A stainless steel "skeleton" goes through all the bronze joints and is welded into the pedestal at the bottom of the statue.

The horse will be finished in 1999, and will be raised in Milan. "It will be exactly 500 years after Leonardo's model was destroyed," Kralik says with pride.

Richard Krentz led the Spirit of Nations team of carvers who created *The Spirit of Lekwammen*, a totem pole which stands 180feet 3inches high.

How they did it

Carvers from seven Native American nations worked together to carve and paint this totem pole which was raised at the 1994 Commonwealth Games in Victoria, British Columbia. Their tree was a 250-year-old western red cedar. "It was the longest cedar log ever logged in British Columbia. We might have set a record for bending stop signs as we went around corners," Krentz jokes. Once the log arrived at the carving site, artists got down to business, using traditional adzes and gouges (cutting and sculpting tools) like those used by carvers over hundreds of years along the coast of the Pacific northwest. "Originally artists used beaver teeth on a stick," says Krentz, "but adzes work better."

Krentz's special pride is the Spirit of Nations figure of an adult with a child. "It says that our hope is in the future, in children." Children helped with the carving, especially the eagle at the very top of the pole. The pole was carved flat on the ground, before it was raised. "If we work together with love and respect, anything's possible," says Krentz.

 ## Largest Painting

This painting of Elvis Presley took up 76,726 square feet of Tybee Island, Georgia. It was painted by students at Savannah College of Art and Design.

How they did it

A great painting of a tiny postage stamp? That's right. Savannah College of Art and Design student Ivan Reyes designed the U.S. postage stamp. Then he helped the school transfer his design to a parking lot on Tybee Island. Local people and teachers and students from the college got together to complete the design with gallons and gallons and gallons of paint.

The biggest origami bird measured 52 feet 6 inches tall, with a wingspan 117 feet wide. People from Cunma, Maobachi, Japan, folded it together from a huge sheet of paper.

Bop But Don't Drop

Tap. Leap. Hop. Bop.
Dance your way to the top.

🏆 Longest Tap Dance

Rosie Radiator and her team of 11 dancers from her school, Rad Taps, tap danced 9.61 miles around San Francisco, California.

How they did it

Rosie Radiator has become internationally famous in the tap dancing world because of her method of tap dancing. "It's called radical tap," she says, "because you relax your legs from the knee down, wear loose shoes, and trick the sounds out of your feet."

Rosie got the idea of trying to set a Guinness record in 1976, when she tapped across the Golden Gate Bridge to celebrate the 200th birthday of the U.S. "People said they wanted to join me. So I started working on a way to dance long distances," she says. "Now, with radical tap, we can look good and be safe on many different surfaces across the city. We can dance on manhole covers, curbs, whatever!" The record-breaking tap dance was choreographed, with steps designed for every minute, and the dancers tapped in unison, matching each other's moves.

TRY THIS!

Want to match Rosie's moves? "Do your own thing," Rosie says. "Make up your own steps. The magic of tap is in your natural movement. Try tapping in the bus station, in the kitchen, in the bathroom, everywhere. " Practice a while... then see how far you can go!

Biggest Chicken Dance

A Chicken Dance that included 72,000 people pretending to be chickens took place at the Canfield Fair in Canfield, Ohio.

How they did it

People who came to the Canfield Fair on Sunday, September 1, 1996, had already heard the fair would be "something to crow about." They had heard the TV and radio ads asking them to come do the famous Chicken Dance. They had seen the giant inflatable rooster set up for the fair's 150th anniversary.

At exactly three o'clock, people in concession booths shut their doors and came out to dance. Fire trucks raised their ladders, and firemen in "cherry pickers" demonstrated the Chicken Dance. Cheerleaders from area high schools stood on top of booths and cars to lead the crowd. Then the music started over the fair's big loudspeakers. The crowd flapped their elbows like wings. They shook their "tail feathers." They squawked like chickens. And together they broke the record.

Most Grand Jete's

This photo shows what a grand jete´ looks like. You can imagine how it feels to do five or six in a row. Wayne Sleep completed 158 grands jete´s (big leaps) in two minutes in Gateshead, England.

EXTRA
Two-Step

Travis Tritt sang "T-R-O-U-B-L-E" as 3,770 people danced in the largest country line dancing ever, in Redwood City, California.

EXTRA Long

The longest dancing dragon stretched 5,550 feet from nose to tail. It took 610 people to make this dragon dance. The dance took place at Tiantan, Beijing China.

Celebrate!

**Are these the world's greatest parties?
Judge for yourself!**

 Most Jack-o-Lanterns

People in the town of Keene, New Hampshire, got together
to carve 13,044 jack-o-lanterns for Halloween, 1996.

How they do it

There are more jack-o-lanterns in Keene every year than
there are people living there. But it hasn't always been
that way. In the early 1990s, downtown Keene seemed
empty to Nancy Sporborg. "It's an amazingly beautiful
town, but there were more and more empty storefronts.
I knew that if I wanted to keep some life in our downtown
I would have to do something about it." Sporborg decided
to organize a Harvest Festival, and a pumpkin-carving
contest to go with it. Then she got the idea of trying to
set a Guinness record. There wasn't any record in the
book, but Sporborg got the go-ahead to try it.

Keene carved 4,818 jack-o-lanterns the first year.
Every Halloween, the town sets out to break the record
all over again. Local farmers donate pumpkins, and
everyone in the area gets out their best ideas. The result
is an astonishing number of smiling, frowning, laughing
and growling jack-o-lanterns. "They carve faces, names,
even company logos," Sporborg says. "Each person
gets the opportunity to bring a piece of themselves
downtown."

Extra Furry

The Dublin Zoo in Dublin, Ireland, hosted the world's
largest teddy bear picnic: 33,573 bears – and their
owners – joined in.

Longest Paper Chain

A paper chain 40.67 miles long was made by students from the University of Missouri-Rolla. It had 450,000 links.

How to do it

The University students got the guidelines from Guinness before they started planning their record break. (See page 64.) Others were already working on the paper chain record. Genevieve Grimes, 17, was one of a team of girl scouts from Wernerville, Pennsylvania who set their own paper chain world record. "You only have 24 hours,"

What's the most important part of setting a paper chain record? "Organization," says Genevieve. It helps to cut the paper loops ahead of time, find a work space, get paper and other supplies, and find people to help with food, errands, and music during the event. The Scouts' record was broken by the University of Missouri students. And others (below) are already practicing their skills. "You have to practice, and get a lot of sleep the night before." advises Genevieve.

TRY THIS!

The most-sung song is "Happy Birthday to You," written by Mildred Hill and Patty Smith Hill. Someone's been singing it every day since the day it came out in 1893.

Going to the Dogs

Wow! Man's best friend is good at many things. Here are just a few doggy records. Bow wow!

 Largest Dog Walk

"Pooches on Parade", held in October, 1996, in Manchester, Connecticut, was the largest dog walk ever. 1,086 dogs walked their owners three miles around a city park.

How they did it

"Pooches on Parade" was organized by Amy Schuster, event manager at Fidelco, which raises and trains guide dogs. "We know a lot of people with dogs!" says Amy. Setting the record was still a lot of work.

Amy called Guinness six months before the record attempt, and learned that the record was then 328. So she tried to gather 600 walkers. Then, three months before the "parade" began, she learned that a new record had been set at 673. "We sent letters to everyone we knew, inviting them to come walk their dogs. We got to work planning the required three-mile loop, setting up a water station, and finding a vet. We needed to have one dog per person – and all the dogs had to have their shots. Whew!"

Fastest Dog Team

In 1995, Doug Swingley's team finished the 1,150-mile Iditarod Race faster than anyone ever: 9 days, 2 hours, 42 minutes, and 19 seconds. He was the first "musher" from outside Alaska ever to win the race.

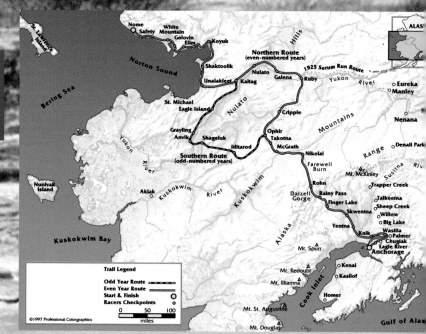

EXTRA Teensy

Big Boss is the world's smallest dog. On his first birthday, he was 4 7/10 inches tall, 5 1/10 inches long, and weighed 1 lb. 1 oz.

TRY THIS!

Josh, a 16-year-old terrier mix from Glen Burnie, Maryland, had been petted by more than 460,000 people by May, 1997. Can your dog beat that?

JOSH for President

Most Guide Dogs Trained

The Seeing Eye, in Morristown, New Jersey, has placed more than 12,000 guide dogs with owners – more than any other organization. Guide Dogs for the Blind, in San Rafael, California, placed 339 dogs in 1996 – the record for a single year.

How they do it

Guide dogs begin their training as puppies. They live with families for 18 months, and are cared for, trained, and "socialized" – taken into many different situations. "They get used to people, cars, trucks, and noise," says Carol Grey of The Seeing Eye. Often, children are puppy trainers, doing basic obedience training and taking the dogs out to "empty" them.

Then the dog works for four months with a Seeing Eye trainer, learning to deal with four commands – left, right, forward, and hup-hup (hurry up). "The dogs learn 'intelligent disobedience' then," says Grey. They learn not to obey a command if it leads to danger. After that the dog trains for 20 to 27 days with the person who will become its owner. On graduation day, everyone comes – puppy trainers, adult trainers, new owners, and the new guide dog!

How they do it

The Iditarod is run every March in Alaska, from Anchorage to Nome. The map shows the route the mushers take in even (northern trail) and odd (southern trail) years. Swingley's record-setting race was run over the southern trail. "Race conditions were really fast," Swingley recalls, "and the dog team was in top condition." He used 16 dogs, including co-leaders Vic and Elmer, and didn't need to replace any dogs for injuries. "It all came together," he says. "I decided to make a go for it."

Swingley wasn't aware that he and his dogs were moving extra fast. "The main thing is the competition, he says. "I was just trying to get in first." The Iditarod was established in memory of a great dog-sled race against time, when mushers carried a special medicine that would stop a diptheria epidemic in Nome. Swingley's dog sled sped through flat tundra, mountains, and frozen rivers, but his mind was not on the scenery. "My favorite place along the route is the finish line.!"

Fur, Feathers, and Fins

Otters and other residents of the Monterey Bay Aquarium – are up to their ears in records. But it wasn't easy getting 364,593 sea creatures under one roof!

Most Species

At last count, the Monterey Bay Aquarium in Monterey, California, housed 571 species of animals and plants. They've got mammals (like this otter), birds and amphibians, reptiles, invertebrates, plants, and – oh, yes! – fish. There are plenty of people around, too: since opening in 1984, more than 21 million people have visited – more than any other aquarium in the U.S.

Extra Wide
You can see these sea nettles through the world's largest aquarium window. It measures 958.8 square feet and weighs 78,000 pounds.

How they did it

The Aquarium sits right in Monterey Bay. If all the water were sucked out of the bay, you'd see terrain from hills and meadows to canyons two miles deep. The Bay hides all this – as well as great numbers of creatures that live in the shallows, watery canyons, and the open sea beyond.

So, how do they get into the Aquarium? Most swim in through its gills, great openings that allow the tide to wash through the tanks. Other aquariums can't use the open-sea system, because the water nearby is polluted.

Tiny eggs and spores (like seeds for animals) flow into the aquarium, stay there, and grow up. Larger creatures – like orphaned baby sea otters and birds – have to be brought in by hand. Jellyfish, crabs, eels, and bat rays are scooped up in nets by people called collectors. Still bigger fish–such as sharks and yellow fin tuna – are caught with a hook and line then brought into the aquarium in special tanks or slings.

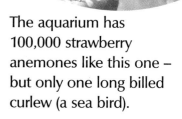

The aquarium has 100,000 strawberry anemones like this one – but only one long billed curlew (a sea bird).

The aquarium needs a shark.
Any volunteers from the ocean?

The sling takes the shark out of the water, into a holding tank, then into the aquarium.

How he did it

"Once I was swimming next to a deep water shark. I swam in front of it with a big hoop net. The boat pulled the net, and the shark ate it out at the other end. So I swam down with a line with a hook. I put it in the shark's mouth, set my heels in the sand, and let the boat pull it up. It gets your heart beating!" – John O'Sullivan, Senior Collector.

A visitor gets a shark's - eye view of the new tank.

TRY THIS!

A gold fish named Fred lived 41 years Can your goldfish top that?

DON'T TRY THIS!

The strongest animal bite ever measured is the dusky shark's: 132 pounds of force, or 22 tons of pressure at the tip of the teeth. But...the bite of the great white shark has yet to be tested.

G.R.O.S.S.*

*(Guinness Records of Shocking Size)

Gross or great? You be the judge, after reading these creepy-crawly records.

Most Venomous Snake

Hydrophis belcheri, from the Timor Sea (in the South Pacific) is 100 times more venomous than any land snake.

How they do it

To measure how toxic (deadly) a snake's venom is, scientists milk the snake and check to see how much venom it takes to kill a mouse. The snake that kills with the smallest amount of venom owns the record.

But there aren't any mice swimming in the Timor Sea. What kind of animal is *Hydrophis belcheri* up against? Nothing special. George Zug of Smithsonian Institute says, "Snakes aren't venomous for defense, but for capturing food. It's an advantage to the snake not to have to track its prey or hang onto it for a long time to kill it. Having strong venom prevents damage to the snake."

Longest Flea Jump

A cat flea (*Clenocephalides felis*) can jump as far as 34 inches.

How they do it

A tiny flea jumps 130 times its own height. Fleas come down hard, too: they land with a force 200 times the normal force of gravity.

They have extra long, strong thigh muscles that propel them off the earth – or off a dog.

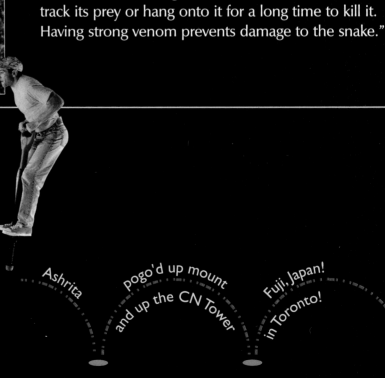

Ashrita pogo'd up mount and up the CN Tower Fuji, Japan! in Toronto!

Largest Termite Mound

A colony of termites built a mound that stood 28 feet 6 inches tall. It was found in Somalia in 1968.

How they do it

A termite mound, like a beehive or an anthill, is as organized as a farm or factory. The termites use chewed-up vegetable material, mixed with dirt, clay, or droppings, to build their giant mounds.

Why do the termites need such big houses? The termites get into the mounds through long underground tunnels guarded by soldier termites. They stay safe deep inside, leaving the soldiers to fight off invading ants or other attackers.

Another reason is food. Inside, worker termites grow fungus. Their fungus gardens are wet, dark areas where bacteria in vegetable matter grows into mold. The gardens grow at ground level, near the cell where the queen termite lives and the chambers where termite larva (babies) are born and raised. Up above are air ducts that keep cool air coming in and warm air going out, as well as "attics" that store spare vegetable material.

EXTRA Long
A worm 22 feet long was found in 1937 in South Africa.

Make a human centipede! The largest centipede was made up of 1,665 humans from the University of Guelph, Canada, on September 6, 1996. The rules: walk 98.5 feet with ankles tied together – and with nobody falling down.

EXTRA Big
A male goliath bird-eating spider (*Theraphosa blondi*) with a leg span of 11.02 inches was collected at Rio Cavro, Venezuela, in April 1965. The spider lives on the ground of the rain forest, waiting for lunch to come near: a mouse, an insect, or even a bird. It leaps on it, using its pedipalps (grabbers near the mouth) to hold the victim. Venom from the spider's fangs paralyzes the prey, and a special liquid from the stomach turns it to mush.

Natural Disasters

People just naturally like to know about records. Before the 20th century, it was difficult to measure natural events. Were there record-breakers before the measurements began? We'll never know!

Greatest Explosion

The eruption of Krakatoa, a volcanic island in Indonesia, caused an explosion 26 times as powerful as the largest hydrogen bomb ever exploded. It happened August 27, 1883, and was heard across 1/13 of Earth's surface.

How it did it

Long ago, Krakatoa was close to 6,000 feet high and covered 18 square miles. It exploded four times during 1883. The third pop is the record-holder. Experts believe that the first two explosions caused the volcano's walls to collapse. Sea water rushed into the hot cone and turned to steam. The steam built up inside the volcano until pressure – combined with the activity of the hot lava rushing up from a vent in the earth's crust – caused the gigantic explosion.

The energy Krakatoa let off equalled about 200 mega tons of TNT. The big blow destroyed two-thirds of the island, including 163 villages.

EXTRA New

An island in Tonga (in the South Pacific) is so new it hasn't been named. The island – just 12 acres – was formed by lava from an underwater volcano. The lava mountain gew higher and higher until it poked through the ocean in 1995. This is how Hawaii – and most other Pacific island groups – were formed.

EXTRA Shocking

The Boston Museum of Science has the world's largest Van de Graaff generator. Robert Van de Graaff built it to study atoms by producing electricity. The big generator (37 feet high) can produce 2.5 million volts of electricity and lightning bolts 15 feet long.

Will Ashrita meet disaster? Wait and

Longest Tornado Track

[T]ornado that hit Missouri, Illinois, and Indiana on
[Ma]rch 18, 1925, stayed on the ground for 219 miles.
[It a]lso caused the most deaths (695), lasted the longest
[(3.5] hours) and destroyed the greatest area (164 square
[mil]es). Its funnel – the widest ever – was more than a
[mil]e wide. At 73 mph, it was the third fastest.

[H]ow they do it

[Tw]isters may happen when a cold front of air comes close
[beh]ind warm weather. They begin with air that flows up
[fro]m a thunderstorm and drop closer to the ground as
[a f]unnel-shaped cloud of high wind and low pressure.
[Fall]ing rain or hail feeds air to the tornado, making it
[swi]rl tighter and faster.

    The Fujita-Pearson scale for damaging winds is
[use]d to measure tornadoes. Each tornado gets three
[sco]res. A tornado that scores 5 (the highest) on the scale
[has] winds of 261-318 mph. The record tornado above
[sco]red only 1 for wind speed on the scale. But its path
[len]gth and width both scored 5's. This was a 1,5,5 tornado.

On July 4, 1995, 38 people were
struck by one bolt of lightning.
They had been waiting to watch
fireworks in Castalia, North
Carolina. All 38 survived.

 ## Strongest Earthquake

The earthquake that rocked Chile on May 22, 1960,
measured 9.5 on the Mw (moment magnitude) scale
and 8.3 on the Ms (surface magnitude) scale. A quake
in Alaska on March 27, 1964, measured 9.3 on the
Mw scale and 8.4 on the Ms or Richter scale.

How they do it

Earthquakes happen when pieces of the Earth's crust
called plates move or collide beneath the ground. The
shock can be measured as the strength of the impact
(moment magnitude) or as waves that spread out from
the earthquake center (surface magnitude). With quakes
above 8 on the Ms scale, scientists trust the Mw scale most.

EXTRA Destructive

The Los Angeles earthquake
of January 17, 1994, caused
the most expensive
destruction of any in
U.S. history – close
to $20 billion.
This photo
shows part
of the Santa
Monica
Freeway.

Quest to the Past

The Earth keeps secrets to its past. Scientists get down and dirty to solve ancient mysteries – using rocks, ash, bones, and even teeth as clues.

Largest Rock

The Aborigine people of Australia call this rock Uluru. Others call it Ayers Rock. Either way, Aussies say it's a "bonza" (great) rock! At 1.5 miles long and one mile wide, Uluru rises 1,143 feet – as high as a 100-story skyscraper.

How it does it

Uluru is sandstone, which forms at the bottom of a heavy weight of sand. As the sand on top blew or washed away, Uluru was uncovered. To the Aborigines, Uluru is a magic, sacred place where creation began. Part of its mystical mood come from its odd shapes, markings, and colors. Arkose, a material in Uluru's sandstone, rusts when it's exposed to air. In some lights, Uluru looks blue; in others, it appears red or orange.

EXTRA Old

Teddy the pony is at least 55 years old, says his owner, Katherine Pennington. No one's sure of his exact age, because a pony's teeth stop changing after 45 years. Too bad Teddy can't talk! "There's a lot of stuff in his head that I'd love to know," says Pennington.

Biggest Dinosaur

Carcharonosaurus saharicus (shark-toothed reptile from the Sahara desert) was 45 feet long from nose to tail, and had a skull 5 feet and 4 inches long.

How he did it

Would you know you'd found the world's largest dinosaur from digging up toe bones? Dr. Paul Sereno found *Carcharonosaurus* toes scattered over 100 miles of desert in Morocco. Then he came across a round bone the size of a softball. "I've studied dinosaur bones so much, I knew it was the back end of a predatory dinosaur's skull." So, where was the front end?

Sereno realized that the break in the bone was fresh (only about 20 years old). He looked up at the cliff above him, and there, sticking out of the rock, was the front end. Back home in his laboratory, Sereno found the age of his dinosaur. He used radiocarbon dating, which measures the energy coming from the atoms that make up fossilized bone. "*Carcharonosaurus* lived 90 million years ago," says Sereno, in awe. "As I worked on the skull, I just kept imagining this animal when it was alive."

Oldest Footprints

1. Mary Leakey, working in Tanzania in 1978, found the oldest proof that human ancestors walked erect (standing up straight) as long as 3.7 million years ago.
2. Dr. Tom Dillehay, working in Chile in 1995, found the oldest signs that people lived in the Americas – 12,500 years ago, much earlier than anyone thought. In both cases, the clues that led to the claims were footprints.

How they did it

Archaeologists in Mary Leakey's camp were having a play fight with dried elephant dung. One fell down, and noticed odd markings on the ground: dents from raindrops that fell into ash millions of years earlier. The group stopped playing and started studying the ash ground, now rock-hard. After two years of searching, Mary Leakey uncovered human footprints. She followed the tracks of a man, woman and child as they walked across an African field millions of years ago.

There was no clue that humans lived in North or South America earlier than 11,500 years ago, until archaeologists found Monte Verde, Chile, a settlement near the Pacific Ocean. A child's footprint beside a fireplace caught Tom Dillehay's imagination. Like Leakey and Sereno, he used radiocarbon dating to find the age of the ash.

Dillehay's discovery opened up a new mystery. A glacier covered North America from about 20,000 years ago to 13,000 years ago. Experts believe the first people in America came over the frozen Bering Strait from Asia. Either the people who lived in Monte Verde came south just as the glacier melted (going 10,000 miles in an incredibly short time) or their ancestors came before the glacier. The answer lies in clues not yet found.

TRY THIS!

Guinness has a new record category, but no record holder yet. We're looking for the oldest person to have milk teeth (baby teeth). Could it be you or someone you know? (See page 64.)

Sounds Amazing

How loud is a sound? It depends on where it comes from...where it goes...what it passes on its way.

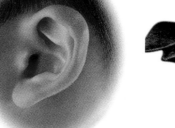

 Loudest Animal Sound

The blue whale communicates in moans, sending out low-frequency sounds that carry up to 530 miles away. These huge moans have been measured at 188 decibels.

EXTRA Long

Blue whales are the biggest animal ever to live on Earth – up to 100 feet in length and 180 tons (as much as 27 adult elephants).

How they do it

Whales don't have vocal cords, and their blowholes don't make noise. So how do they make groans louder than jet engines?

Scientists think maybe the noise comes from empty spaces (like human sinuses) inside their heads. The whales may push air from one space to another so quickly that they make an explosion of sound.

Sounds travel five times faster underwater than they do in air. And sound doesn't lose its energy underwater. It bounces off the undersurface of the water and off the ocean bottom, and just keeps on going.

People who study whale calls find patterns like the verses of songs. Whales may use sound to form pictures in their minds the way humans use their vision. Through sound, whales may be able to picture objects or maps. As blue whales swim, they can stay "together" through sound - even though they're 100 miles apart.

Clapping

V. Jeyarama holds the world record for continuous clapping: 58 hours, 9 minutes. That's 160 claps per minute, audible at 120 feet away. This photo shows Ashrita Furman, the U.S. record holder. He clapped for 50 minutes.

How he did it

The first time Ashrita Furman tried to break the clapping record, he failed. The place he chose to clap – New York's Lincoln Center – was too noisy. The judges couldn't hear him.

So Ashrita tried again. He stood on one side of a stream, and his judges stood on the other. Sound travels better across water than it does across pavement. "I didn't have to clap as hard, so I could go on longer," says Ashrita. "I made it!"

TRY THIS!

Annalisa Wray, of Belfast, Northern Ireland, holds the shouting record. Her yell hit 121.7 decibels. What did she yell? "QUIET!"

Most Acute Hearing

Bats can hear more than any other terrestrial (land) animal. Some bats can hear sounds from 20 kHz to 250 kHz – a huge range that includes many sound frequencies (measured as the length of time between sound waves).

How they do it

Bats use echolocation to get around and catch prey. They chirp high-pitched sounds that echo – bounce off – objects. The echoes tell them how far away something is, how big it is, what shape it is, and how it's moving. Echolocation – also called sonar – helps bats navigate even in the darkest caves. The sounds that they hear have such high frequency they're called ultrasonic. Dolphins, which also use echolocation, can hear sounds at 280 kHz. And humans? We're way out of the range, able to hear sounds almost as high as 20 kHz.

EXTRA Strumming
The largest acoustic guitar is on display at The Exploratory, in Bristol, England. It's 28 feet 5 inches long, and 3 feet 2 inches deep. You can play it, if you've got a really big pick!

Light Fantastic

If people could travel as light travels, we'd zip in powerful waves across huge spaces. We'd bounce off mirrors and lakes quicker than a blink of the eye... We'd shimmer among the raindrops and show off all our colors.

Farthest-Reaching Lights

The Empire State Building in New York City has lights that can be seen from 80 miles away on the ground and 300 miles away by aircraft.

How they do it

The Empire State Building's lights haven't always been so bright. Though the building was first lit up in 1931, the lights were redesigned for the 200th birthday of the United States in 1976. Douglas Leigh designed red, white, and blue lights for the celebration and planned the switch to bright white lights that came on afterward.

From the 72nd floor to the top of the TV antenna, 1,454 feet above the ground, the building is lit by 204 metal halide lamps, 1,100 fluorescent lamps, and 18 halo lights. The lamps each create candle power of 1,000 watts each. Powerful? Yes, but the building's great height helps. Once you go beyond 80 miles away, the building and its lights are hidden by the curve of the Earth.

For special occasions (such as Martin Luther King, Jr.'s birthday or a New York Yankees World Series win) the Empire State shines different colors. Colored lights don't travel as far. Pure white light – which hasn't been broken down into different colors – travels the farthest.

Longest-Lasting Rainbow

A rainbow arched over Sheffield, England, for six hours on March 14, 1994.

How it did it

Light travels from its source (the sun or a bulb) at 184,000 miles per hour, If the light can't go through something it goes around it, making a shadow. But light can pass through many substances – air, water, paper, glass.

What light goes through changes it. The light may get bent, or *reflected*. It may get broken up into different colors, or *refracted*. A rainbow happens when light passes through water, which refracts it.

If you have ever made rainbows in the water of a backyard hose, you know that if you move to one side the rainbow disappears. To see the rainbow, you have to be positioned just right. If you could keep the stream of water, the sun, and your eye at the same angles to one another, you could keep that rainbow going as long as you wanted – and challenge the longest-lasting natural rainbow with your homemade one.

Biggest Kaleidoscope

The Kaatskill Kaleidoscope in Mount Tremper, New York, measures 56 feet 3 inches long, just about as long as – yes, that's what it is – the silo of a barn.

How they did it

A big kaleidoscope needs big mirrors. This one has a pyramid of mirrors 37 1/2 feet high. No, mirrors don't usually come that large. Kaleidoscope designer Charles Karadimos made them of reflecting material used for the outside of buildings. The mirror pyramid reflects computer video paintings done by artists Isaac and Raphael Adams. The light from the pictures bounces from one mirror to another to form a pattern that seems to turn as the video changes.

Kaleidoscope visitors don't peer inside; they just walk in. They stand at the bottom of the silo and look up into the inside of the pyramid. What they see looks like a giant marble of patterns 50 feet wide. As they watch, they listen to special music composed to go with the show. You can bet there are plenty of oohs and aahs.

EXTRA Eagle-Eyed

The Keck telescope, the world's largest, stands on Mauna Kea, in Hawaii. Andy Parala has used the Keck to see far-away galaxies and the farthest-away object, a quasar. How far is far? "Thirteen billion light years away. Thirteen billion years is how long the light has been traveling to get to us. A giant telescope is like a time machine. When you look at it you're looking at something that happened eons and eons ago."

TRY THIS!

To spy Sirius A (*Alpha Canis Majoris*) – the dog star, just look for the brightest star in the sky. Sirius is 24 times as bright as the sun and is 8.64 light years away.

Rocks in Space

They're pieces of old planets or stars. They're flying fireballs. And you might see them in your own backyard.

Largest and Smallest Asteroids

Now orbiting the sun: 1 Ceres, 596 miles in diameter, and 1993KA2, just 16 feet around.

How they do it

The main asteroid belt between Mars and Jupiter contains nearly a million pieces of space rock that are at least half a mile in diameter – and many smaller ones. Asteroids in our solar system come from that belt. They float there forever. Or something hits them (not, we hope, the Millenium Falcon). Or they become "rogues", going off on their own to travel around the solar system. Some wind up on Earth as meteors.

Asteroids are what caused the craters on the moon. Because the moon has no atmosphere, it has no defense against asteroids. Earthlings worry that a big meteor could cause great damage here, too. Scientists are working on creating a defense system with lasers or rockets. Big meteors hit only once every 100,000 years, but could hit any time.

Most Comets Discovered

Carolyn Shoemaker has discovered 32 comets, including Shoemaker-Levy 9, which crashed into Jupiter several years after she found it.

How she does it

When astronomer Eugene Shoemaker climbed Palomar Mountain in California to study the sky, his wife Carolyn came along to help him. They'd spend the nights using Palomar's telescope to take photographs of the stars, then go back to their laboratory to study them. And that's where Carolyn found out she had an eye for comets.

Carolyn would study her photographs with a microscope, in hope of finding something that "shouldn't" be there – in other words, not a star or planet. "After a while your mind just says, 'Whoa!'" she says. "I've been blessed with keen eyesight, and I've learned to look at things in a different way. A comet looks like a point of light." To Carolyn Shoemaker, comet-hunting takes sharp eyes, warm clothes, patience – and Oreos. "That's what kept us going on those cold night on Palomar!" That, and the hope of finding new comets.